MILITARY
HUMAN
RESOURCE
ISSUES

MILITARY HUMAN RESOURCE ISSUES:

A MULTINATIONAL VIEW

Edited by:
Lieutenant-Colonel P.J. Johnston
& Dr. Kelly Farley

CANADIAN DEFENCE ACADEMY PRESS

Canadian Defence Academy Press
PO Box 17000 Stn Forces
Kingston, Ontario   K7K 7B4

Produced for the Canadian Defence Academy Press
by 17 Wing Winnipeg Publishing Office.
WPO30888

Cover photos: Combat Camera

Library and Archives Canada Cataloguing in Publication

Military human resource issues : a multinational view / edited by
P.J. Johnston & Kelly Farley.

Produced for the Canadian Defence Academy Press
by 17 Wing Winnipeg Publishing Office.
Issued by: Canadian Defence Academy.
Available also on the Internet.
Includes bibliographical references and index.
ISBN 978-1-100-21718-5
Cat. no.: D2-318/2013E

1. Armed Forces--Personnel management. 2. Recruiting and enlistment. I. Farley, Kelly M. J. (Kelly Matthew John), 1959- II. Johnston, P. John (Pierre John), 1962- III. Canadian Defence Academy IV. Canada. Canadian Armed Forces. Wing, 17

UB146 M54 2013   355.6'1   C2013-980033-6

Printed in Canada.

1 3 5 7 9 10 8 6 4 2

ACKNOWLEDGEMENTS

The editors would like to acknowledge several people who made this publication possible. First, we would like to thank all of the contributors for their exemplary work contained in this book. We would like to thank Lieutenant-Colonel Jeff Stouffer at the Canadian Forces Leadership Institute, for his editorial review, and guidance throughout the publication process. We also wish to acknowledge the stellar work of the Canadian Defence Academy Press, including the staff at the 17 Wing Publishing Office, for transforming our raw manuscript into a finished publication.

Special thanks go to the Director General Military Personnel Research and Analysis (DGMPRA) for administrative support during the editing process and particular thanks to Mr. Jason Dunn and Ms. Samantha Urban for their assistance in developing the glossary and index sections, in addition to their content contributions.

Finally, we would be remiss if not to acknowledge the support provided by all member nations of The Technical Cooperation Panel (TTCP); that is, the supervisors and managers of all those who spent their valuable time putting this publication together.

PUBLISHER'S PREFACE

The Canadian Defence Academy Press continues to work at its mandate of creating a distinct and unique body of Canadian leadership literature and knowledge that will assist leaders at all levels of the Canadian Forces (CF) to prepare themselves for operations in a complex security environment, as well as to inform the public with respect to the contribution of CF service personnel to Canadian society and international affairs. Furthermore, it is maintaining its contributions to the international discussion of military issues by introducing the latest in its series of international volumes. This most recent work, *Military Human Resource Issues: A Multinational View*, is the latest in this collection.

The modernization of the military throughout the world has resulted in an increased pressure to recruit and retain professional military members, while at the same time ensuring the proper balance between force structure and the imperative of taking care of personnel through robust well-being programs. As such, this book provides an examination of military human resources at the international level and showcases different approaches to managing these changing requirements.

Significantly, the physical and mental challenges of operations are now housed within the context of whole of government operations and/or joint, allied or multinational forces – each layer requiring additional skill sets from the modern soldier. Importantly, this volume analyzes the changing role of military human resources in response to the considerable dynamic nature of modern military operations, both domestically and abroad. It looks at complex issues such as: recruiting and selection, testing, assessment methodology, performance, and well-being.

Once again, CDA Press is pleased to present this book, which we believe will be a valuable addition to the body of knowledge on the profession of arms. As always, your comments and suggestions are welcomed.

Bernd Horn
Colonel, OMM, MSM, CD, PhD
Editor-in-Chief
CDA Press

TABLE OF CONTENTS

TABLE OF CONTENTS

FOREWORD

The operational capability of any military is largely dependant on its people. Whether it is war fighting, peacekeeping, or assisting our communities in times of need, the key to success is having the right personnel with the right qualifications in the right job when we need them there. Achieving these goals is a responsibility shared by personnel specialists and all CF leaders.

Senior military leaders, including officers and non-commissioned officers (NCOs) must be able to make informed decisions regarding military personnel and the way to do that is through a robust understanding of the personnel management system. This includes understanding personnel generation; that is, organizational structure, recruiting, selection, training and development, and performance evaluation. In addition, all leaders should be familiar with the principles of career management, compensation, benefits and employee health and welfare, which are essential to look after the personal aspirations and well-being of their people. And finally, commanders and other leaders need to have an appreciation for the impact that military life has on the military family and how that, in turn, affects the performance of our people. These are the tenets of Military Human Resource Management (HRM), and the focus of this volume.

This publication is a significant achievement by the contributing authors, The Technical Cooperation Panel, Technical Panel 3, and the Canadian Defence Academy Press. It demonstrates the power of collaborative efforts to compile knowledge, expertise and resources to produce a top shelf reference for military leaders around the world. The dedication and professionalism of these individuals and groups is commendable.

Military Human Resource Issues: A Multinational View is a collection of short chapters that focus on various HRM topics that are particularly relevant to the military organization. The selected readings cover topics from across the spectrum of HRM, from recruiting and selection, to personnel production planning, to caring for military families. As such, I strongly recommend this book for all military leaders.

Rear-Admiral A. Smith
Chief Military Personnel
Canadian Forces

PREFACE

Military Human Resource Issues: A Multinational View, is a compilation of works from members of the Technical Cooperation Panel, Technical Panel 3 (TP3). TTCP has a long history of cooperative and collaborative research, and this book demonstrates the on-going value of this partnership, through the 13 chapters written by researchers from Australia, Canada, New Zealand, the United Kingdom and the United States of America. This collection of chapters broadly covers the spectrum of the personnel production and management system. I believe that all military Human Resources (HR) practitioners, including junior and senior leadership, will want to keep a copy on their bookshelf as a quick reference.

Personnel in any organization represent an essential resource that must be managed just like financial resources, technological resources, information resources, etc. In fact, human resources are the foundation upon which all others are built. If organizations do not manage their human resources well – that is, recruit, select, train, and look after the well-being of their people, then those people will not take care of all the other resources, which are essential to organizational and operational effectiveness. Indeed, the effective management of human resources is key to organizational success.

These short chapters will provide valuable insights into the science and practice of human resource management that are meant as a resource for senior military HR practitioners. Chapters 1 to 8 explain the basics of production planning, recruiting, and selection. In particular, the reader will see an overview of Job Analysis, which is the basis of any personnel production system. A very readable chapter on the complexities of modelling and simulation will shed some light on the magic behind production planning in military organizations. In Chapter 3 you will read a U.S. perspective on the importance of finding high quality applicants, while balancing off the high costs of recruiting. Chapters 4 to 8 are all focused on how we can select the right person for the job, through selection testing methodologies in general, intelligence testing, occupational personality testing, assessment centres, and online testing methodologies. In Chapter 9, the topic changes focus to measuring performance of military personnel, a topic that is essential for all leaders to understand. Chapters 10 and 11 may be two of the most important chapters, not focused on military personnel as much as on their families, looking at the challenges associated with being a military family member, and the impact of a spousal career on the military member. Of course, no discussion of HRM would be complete without a look at how to retain talent; therefore, you will find such a discussion in chapter 12. Finally, we are presented with an excellent chapter on surveys and how to use them in the science and practice of HRM.

Military Human Resource Issues: A Multinational View is the most recent CDA press publication that brings together an international group of researchers to provide a series of chapters relevant to all military HR practitioners. The authors and publication team should be applauded for compiling this compendium of well-researched and well-written papers on important HRM topics, presented in terms that the practitioner will appreciate and relate to.

Susan Truscott

Director General Military Personnel Research and Analysis, Canadian Forces

Canadian National Representative –
Human Resources and Performance (HUM) Group, TTCP

CHAPTER 1

JOB ANALYSIS AND
COMPETENCY MODELLING

BRIAN TATE, CHAD I. PEDDIE, and TONIA S. HEFFNER
U.S. Army Research Institute for the Behavioral and Social Sciences

INTRODUCTION

Behind nearly all effective applicant selection tools, performance appraisal systems, training programs, and job restructuring efforts is an effective job analysis. Job analysis refers to the process of identifying and documenting what job incumbents do (their tasks or activities), under what conditions they perform, the kinds of technology they use, and who they are, which is usually defined in terms of their knowledge, skills, abilities, and other characteristics (KSAOs). Of particular concern are job characteristics and worker attributes that distinguish effective from ineffective performance within the context of a single position, job, or group of jobs.[1] The goal of any job analysis is to provide an accurate and comprehensive assessment of a job. Without the information that a job analysis provides, it is unlikely that any of the personnel functions listed above would be successful.

The information obtained through job analysis is not limited to use in selection, training, performance management, and many other personnel efforts.[2] Depending on aspects of an organization (e.g., industry and size) and the particular personnel activity in question, job analysis is a legal necessity. Activities based on a job analysis are more likely to

1

withstand possible legal challenges.[3] Even in organizations not legally bound by anti-discrimination laws, valid personnel management activities begin with an effective job analysis.

JOB ANALYSIS METHODOLOGY

The most appropriate method of conducting a job analysis depends on several factors, including the reason for the analysis (in other words, what the information will be used for), the availability of time and other resources, and a consideration of potential legal implications. Characteristics of the job in question, the people who perform the job, and the organization to which it belongs are also important. Although job analyses may differ along several dimensions, traditional analyses tend to follow a process depicted in Figure 1.1. Activities that take place during the planning stages of an analysis focus on defining project goals, timelines, and other information that can be used to develop a plan for project execution. This stage is typically followed by attempts to compile basic information about a job. After job information is collected, these data are then revised, validated, and/or brought up-to-date. Finally, the results of an analysis should be put into a form that makes them useful to an organization. Key parts of the job analysis process are discussed below.

Several decisions must be made prior to beginning a job analysis. Three of the most important decisions include: work versus worker-oriented descriptors; sources of information; and from whom to collect the information.

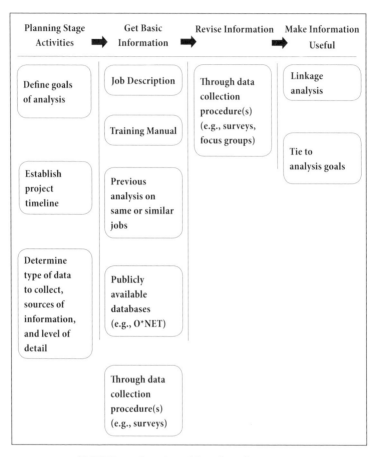

FIGURE 1.1: Overview of the Job Analysis Process

PLANNING STAGE DECISIONS

Work versus Worker-Oriented Descriptors

Some job analyses techniques focus on the work that a job incumbent performs (work-oriented approaches), some focus on characteristics of effective job incumbents (worker-oriented approaches), some incorporate both kinds of information (hybrid approaches)[4] and a more recent approach is that of personality-based job analysis. A work-oriented analysis typically features the collection of task or activity statements that describe the actions or behaviours involved in performing a job.[5] A worker-oriented approach focuses upon the attributes of job incumbents that lead to successful performance.[6] The worker-oriented characteristics are typically organized into the KSAOs mentioned above. In contrast to more traditional job analysis methods, personality-based job analyses attempt to establish links between jobs and the personality factors that correspond with successful performance.

Many job analyses techniques rely on multiple sources of information. For example, hybrid approaches take into account both job tasks and worker attributes. This approach typically features a linkage analysis, which ties task statements to the worker attributes that are important for high performance. A linkage analysis is typically executed by asking job incumbents or other individuals with enough knowledge of a job to be subject matter experts (SMEs) to rate the extent to which each of a set of worker attributes contributes to the performance of a set of tasks.[7] A linkage analysis is a way of determining the job relatedness of KSAOs by highlighting likely relationships between worker attributes and job tasks. Accordingly, results of a linkage analysis can be used as evidence of the job relatedness of the criteria upon which an organization is basing applicant selection and personnel promotion procedures.[8]

Whereas results of work-oriented job analyses are particularly useful for informing training guides and performance evaluations, worker-oriented job analyses can help job and organizational restructuring efforts. Hybrid approaches are particularly relevant for the development of applicant selection procedures, for which it is necessary to know the personal characteristics upon which applicants should be selected and why those characteristics are important.

Sources of information

Regardless of the type of information with which a job analysis is concerned, it will likely involve multiple rounds of information gathering.[9] As reflected in Figure 1.1 above, these rounds can generally be divided into initial information gathering and information revising stages. To gain an initial understanding of a job, a job analyst usually consults sources like training manuals, procedural guides, job descriptions, previous job analyses, and databases of information on jobs, such as the Occupational Information Network, or O*NET.[10] Initial sets of tasks and KSAOs can then be revised through subsequent steps.

In addition to consulting written materials, a job analyst will typically observe and/or talk to job incumbents and other people with knowledge of the job. Below are five methods of information gathering and revision that involve a degree of interaction between a job analyst and a job incumbent or SME. Although the methodologies are discussed separately, to be comprehensive, job analysts often employ a combination of them.[11]

Direct Observation. Direct observation of job incumbents performing their jobs is an obvious way to gather information; this approach, however, has limitations. The primary limitation is that people sometimes tend to alter their behaviour in the presence of an observer typically by working harder or differently than they normally would.[12] This tendency to change behaviour in the presence of an observer may mislead an observer to infer that the behaviours demonstrated are normal and that there are some associated personal attributes that are required to perform the job, when in fact under normal circumstances those behaviours would not have been demonstrated at all. This method is also not appropriate for all jobs. For some jobs, such as emergency medical provider, much can be learned through observation, but for others, such as someone performing computer programming, the data analyst would observe little more than job incumbents sitting at a computer, striking keys.

Critical Incidents. A second approach is to solicit critical incidents from job incumbents and SMEs.[13] This method involves asking incumbents and SMEs to describe actions undertaken by job holders that have resulted in a good or bad outcome. Although collecting such incidents is useful for obtaining examples of behaviours that have led to notable outcomes, it is less effective at obtaining examples of behaviours that result in only moderately good or bad outcomes, those that someone does daily and does not think of as noteworthy or exciting.[14] Thus, the method may not lead to the identification of all relevant behaviors or worker attributes.

Interviews and Focus Groups. A third and related method is to conduct interviews with individuals or discussions with focus groups.[15] Performing a focus group involves assembling a group of incumbents and/or SMEs in order to ask them about the work they perform and/or the KSAOs involved in its performance. The discussions can be unstructured (free flowing) or structured (with planned and pointed questions). Interviews can be conducted in a similar manner but with single individuals. Compared to using critical incidents, focus groups or interviews are more likely to result in examples of behaviours or KSAOs associated with both extreme and moderate outcomes and that are reflective of both day-to-day job performance and performance during peak or extreme situations.[16]

An important consideration with focus groups and interviews is the make-up (i.e. personality, experience, etc.) of the sample of participants. Participants' backgrounds affect what they know about a job and what they report. For example, job incumbents may say that that some characteristics (e.g., educational qualifications) are more important than they are in reality.[17] Thus, it is important to identify a group of individuals who have a great understanding of a job and are unlikely to provide biased information.

Surveys. With the survey method of collecting data, individuals are asked to rate a set of predetermined tasks and/or KSAOs on key attributes, like their importance to the job, how frequently they are performed, and their difficulty.[18] Surveys generally demand less time from participants than interviews or focus groups and make obtaining input from individuals spread over a large geographical area easier. Many job analyses use surveys in conjunction with other methods. For example, someone conducting an analysis may use focus groups to identify an initial set of tasks and ask a larger group of job incumbents to rate the frequency and importance of performing each on a survey in order to determine the most relevant ones.

From Whom to Collect Information

Observation, critical incidents, interviews, focus groups, and surveys can be conducted with several different types of people, including job incumbents and their supervisors, professional job analysts, and anyone else whose knowledge of a job would qualify them as an SME (e.g., technical experts, organizational shareholders, and executive-level leaders).[19] Each type offers advantages and disadvantages. Job incumbents have the most direct experience performing a job but may exaggerate the importance of some KSAOs. Supervisors are knowledgeable of a job but may underestimate the challenges facing incumbents. Job analysts, however have been shown to be knowledgeable of multiple jobs through direct experience, instruction, or advanced study. In fact, research has shown that the input provided by job analysts is more reliable, or consistent, than that provided by other sources;[20] as analysts do not always have direct experience performing the job, however, they may not be aware of some of the informal job requirements. Thus, different groups of individuals may paint different pictures of a job.[21] Consequently, choices regarding the individuals with whom to consult for information about a job are among the most important in the execution of a job analysis.[22]

Depth and Breadth of Job Analysis Information

Information derived from a job analysis can range from very broad and general to very detailed and specific.[23] The most appropriate level of detail depends upon the purpose for the analysis. Whereas a job analysis intended to inform organization-wide change initiatives may be most useful if it focuses on broad-level tasks and attributes, an analysis intended to assist in the development of a new training protocol should focus on tasks and attributes at a more detailed level.

Training of Contributors

Also of importance when planning the path a job analysis will take is the consideration of whether members involved in the effort will receive training. Additionally, determining what content to train, and which methods may be used in the administration of training are important. Although this piece of the process may further tax resources and add to foreseeable deadlines, research focusing on job analysis best practices illustrates the critical need for individuals engaged in the effort to receive some form of training.[24] It is frequently recommended that job raters, including job incumbents, supervisors, and/or analysts are provided with training that presents and explains examples of information being investigated in the analysis and that training regarding the correct completion of surveys and questionnaires be administered.[25] Training initiatives developed for raters typically focus on the reduction of rater biases by providing definitions of rating dimensions, explaining the scale anchors, describing behaviors associated with particular dimensions, providing opportunities for practice, and administration of rater feedback on the practice.[26]

POST-PLANNING STAGES

After a job analysis has been planned from a logistical and method-ological perspective, completing the analysis is a simple matter of ex-ecution. As with all steps of the job analysis process, as an analysis is executed, finalized, and reported, it is most critical that those conduct-ing it remain consistent and true to the organization's intended uses for the analysis. If an organization needs a job analysis as part of an effort to develop an applicant selection program, a job analysis that identifies job tasks but not measurable KSAOs at multiple levels of detail is unlikely to be useful.

COMPETENCY MODELING VS. TRADITIONAL JOB ANALYSIS

Some jobs are more appropriately analyzed with a methodology known as competency modelling, instead of more traditional forms of job analysis.[27] Although there are few inherent differences between the two, i.e., both are defined as procedures for identifying employee characteristics and actions that distinguish exceptional from poor per-formers[28], there are differences in the ways they tend to be conducted. Five qualities that tend to distinguish competency modelling from job analysis include the type of characteristic studied, purpose, level of fo-cus, time orientation, and methodological rigor.

Characteristic of Focus

Competencies tend to be defined as any worker attribute or aspect of worker performance that distinguishes good from poor performance.[29] In practice, competency modelling generally focuses on worker attri-butes at a more general level than does job analysis.[30] As a result, find-ings from competency modelling tend to be highly similar to results of a less detailed worker-oriented job analysis.[31] Table 1.1 highlights similarities and differences between competencies and the tasks and KSAOs resulting from a typical job analysis. As the table shows, competencies tend to be less specific than job analytic information. Job analytic information typically ranges in scale from more specific (e.g., "record facts to prepare reports that document incidents and activities") to more general (e.g., "oral communication"). Thus, although competency modelling and job analysis may result in different kinds of information collected about a job, there is likely to be a degree of overlap between the results of each.

Competencies	Job Analysis Descriptors
Leadership	Record facts to prepare reports that document incidents and activities[a]
Service orientation and delivery	Render aid to accident victims and other persons requiring first aid for physical injuries[a]
Thinking skills	Critical thinking[b]
Personal effectiveness and flexibility	Social perceptiveness[b]
Organization and planning	Oral comprehension[c]
Interpersonal relations	Knowledge of telecommunications systems[d]
Communication	Resolve conflicts and negotiate with others[e]
Motivation	Concern for others[f]

Examples of competencies taken from Catano, Darr, & Campbell's (2007) study of Royal Canadian Mounted Police. Examples of job analysis descriptors taken from O*NET's listing for Police Patrol Officers. [a]Example of job tasks. [b]Example of skills. [c]Example of ability. [d]Example of knowledge. [e]Example of general work activity. [f]Example of work style.

TABLE 1.1: Example Competencies vs. Job Analysis Descriptors

Purpose

Whereas the purpose of job analysis is to describe jobs in enough detail to inform staffing, training, and compensation efforts, competency modelling is better thought of as part of a process of changing, rather than describing, jobs and worker behaviour in some way.[32] For example, competency modelling may be a better choice for a pharmaceutical company that wants to change the process by which its employees receive, fill, and distribute medications. To fulfil this role, competency modelling typically begins by deducting competency labels from an organization's mission statement or description of the desired end-state of its initiative.[33] The extent to which a current workforce possesses those competencies can be estimated and less-than-ideal workforce competency levels can be remedied through restructuring jobs or orienting personnel with examples of competency-exemplifying behaviours.

Level of Focus

Another difference between competency modelling and job analysis is the level of focus. Whereas job analysis tends to focus upon individual jobs or groups of similar jobs, competency modelling efforts have been applied to large groups of jobs, sometimes entire organizations.[34] A competency model's relevance at multiple organizational levels partly stems from the nature of its descriptors. Competencies like those included in Table 1.1 tend to be described in less detail than job analytic information, making them relevant at multiple levels.

Time Orientation

For many efforts, job analysis can be thought as a process of describing positions to inform organizational leaders of the work performed by organizational members; however, competency models may be viewed as more prescriptive.[35] In other words, whereas job analyses may look at what workers currently do in their roles, competency models tend to focus on the prescription of role responsibilities that directly correspond to the strategic mission and vision of the agency employing them.[36] If job analysis or competency modelling results appear to be static, it is because the data collected typically reflects the characteristics and scope of a given position at a given point in time. However, job analysis and competency modelling can take a forward looking approach to analyze jobs, based on changes that are expected, as long as subject matter experts can communicate those expected changes.

Methodological Rigor

Lastly, one of the more important distinctions between competency modelling and job analysis is the extent to which each is perceived to be methodologically sound.[37] Job analysis typically involves multiple rounds of interviews, focus groups, observations, and/or surveys conducted with and administered to carefully screened groups of incumbents and/or SMEs.[38] With competency modelling efforts, organizations often value time-to-completion over the methodological quality of the results.[39] For example, an organization may ask only one group of supervisors to rate the extent to which a set of predetermined competencies contributes to performance. The lack of detailed information and scientifically-sound methodologies found in many competency models may help to explain why they are less likely than job analysis efforts to be used as a basis for legally challengeable personnel activities (e.g., applicant selection).[40]

As this discussion suggests, although competency modelling is not a substitute for job analysis, it can serve some functions more efficiently than job analysis. Competency modelling offers a viable alternative to job analysis for gathering broad-level information about the performance-relevant attributes of job incumbents or an entire workforce, and it can be performed in a way that demands less time and financial resources than job analysis.

The Occupational Information Network

Sponsored by the U.S. Department of Labor, the Occupational Information Network (O*NET) is an electronic database with information on approximately 1000 jobs. O*NET's database is populated according to six information domains: worker characteristics (e.g., abilities), worker requirements (e.g., knowledge), occupation characteristics (e.g., wages), occupational requirements (e.g., generalized work activities), occupation-specific requirements (e.g., equipment), and experience requirements (e.g., training).[41] For many jobs, O*NET provides enough information to either function in place of a job analysis for certain personnel functions (e.g., establishing pay grades and evaluation systems)[42] or be used as input for a subsequent job analysis. For example, a researcher performing a job analysis for a police department may use data from O*NET as an initial set of tasks that officers within a particular department are likely to be asked to perform. The researcher can then revise the list according to results of interviews, focus groups, and/or observations.

A primary limitation of O*NET is that it does not include data on all occupations. In particular, O*NET does not include information on jobs specific to the military (e.g., infantryman). O*NET is not without application to the military however, as research has shown O*NET's methods of data collection, which emphasize the use of automated surveys, have promise for performing job analyses on military jobs.[43]

CHALLENGES ASSOCIATED WITH JOB ANALYSES IN THE U.S. ARMY

Within the U.S. Army, a particularly difficult challenge has been developing a job analysis system that can be consistently applied to the over-200 army occupations and provide sufficient detail about tasks and soldier attributes to inform activities like screening applicants for selection, classifying new personnel to jobs, deciding upon special assignments and promotions, updating training protocols and developing assessments of job performance to use in test validation studies.

An analysis of U.S. Army Special Forces occupations found 47 lower-level attributes of soldiers within these occupations.[44] An assessment of attributes of this number illustrates the problems inherently associated with the job analysis efforts targeted toward an operation of the size and breadth as the U.S. Army. Undertaking an analysis of all the army's jobs would require unlimited time and financial resources. It has been estimated that large civilian organizations (of size and scope significantly less than the army) spend between $150,000 and $4,000,000 annually on job analyses.[45]

Historically, the army has conducted job analyses on a job-by-job basis, executing each in somewhat different manners. As a consequence, although the existing job analyses provide information needed to inform personnel actions specific to a single job, they do not provide enough information at the same broad-level to inform cross-job actions, like developing army-wide assessments of soldiers' job performance, which can be used in promotion decisions and test validation studies. Accordingly, the army has recently begun to consider approaches that emphasize the use of automated surveys to collect data on tasks and soldier attributes at low to high levels of detail. Such an approach would help to ensure that the information collected through job analyses is consistent enough and available at an appropriate level of detail to inform actions involving single and multiple jobs.

SUMMARY

Job analysis is the foundation of any human resource management system. A good job analysis will result in a clear description of the critical tasks and associated knowledge, skills, abilities and other attributes required by job incumbents. Job descriptions provide the vital information required to establish all HR systems such as recruiting, selection, training and development, performance appraisal, promotion decisions, etc. The purpose of these HR functions is to enable managers to make objective, valid and reliable HR decisions that can be legally defended, if questioned. Equally important is the need to ensure the right person is selected for each job, developed, evaluated and rewarded appropriately throughout their career, so that they will be productive and happy at work. A rigorous job analysis will help to achieve all of these aims.

ENDNOTES

1   Michael T. Brannick and Edward L. Levine, *Job Analysis: Methods, Research, and Applications for Human Resource Management in the New Millennium* (Thousand Oaks, CA: Sage Publications, 2002).; Ernest J. McCormick,"Job and Task Analysis," in Marvin D. Dunnette, ed., *Handbook of Industrial and Organizational Psychology* (Chicago, IL: Rand-McNally, 1976), 651-696.; Juan I. Sanchez, "From Documentation to Innovation: Reshaping Job Analysis to Meet Emerging Business Needs," *Human Resource Management Review*, Vol. 4 (1994), 51-74.

2   Herman Aguinis and Kurt Kraiger, "Benefits of Training and Development for Individuals and Teams, Organizations, and Society," *Annual Review of Psychology,* Vol. 60 (2009), 451-474; Society for Industrial and Organizational Psychology, *Principles for the Validation and Use of Personnel Selection Procedures*, 4th ed., (Bowling Green, OH: Author, 2003); Wayne F. Cascio and Herman Aguinis, *Applied Psychology in Human Resource Management*, 6th ed., (Upper Saddle River, NJ: Pearson-Prentice Hall, 2005).

3   Erich C. Dierdorff and Mark A. Wilson, "A Meta-Analysis of Job Analysis Reliability," *Journal of Applied Psychology*, Vol. 88 (2003), 635-646; Paul R. Sackett and Roxanne M. Laczo, "Job and Work Analysis," in Walter C. Borman, Daniel R. Ilgen and Richard J. Klimoski, eds., *Handbook of Psychology: Industrial and Organizational Psychology* (Hoboken, NJ: Wiley, 2003), Vol. 12, 21-37; Juan I. Sanchez and Edward L. Levine, "The Analysis of Work in the 20th and 21st Centuries," In Neil Anderson, Denis S. Ones, Handan K. Sinangil, and Chockalingam Viswesvaran, eds., *Handbook of Industrial, Work and Organizational Psychology* (Thousand Oaks, CA: Sage Publications, 2001), Vol. 1, 71-89.

4   Robert M. Guion, "Analysis of Selection Problems," in *Assessment, Measurement, and Prediction for Personnel Decisions* (Mahwah, NJ: Lawrence Erlbaum Associates, 1998), 47-102; Sackett and Laczo, "Job and Work Analysis."

5   Sackett and Laczo, "Job and Work Analysis".

6   Brannick and Levine, *Job Analysis*; Sackett and Laczo, "Job and Work Analysis".

7   Sackett and Laczo, "Job and Work Analysis".

8   Guion, "Analysis of Selection Problems".

9   Ibid.

10   Ibid.

11   Sanchez and Levine, "The Analysis of Work".

12   Guion, "Analysis of Selection Problems".

13   John C. Flanagan, "The Critical Incident Technique," *Psychological Bulletin,* Vol. 51 (1954), 327-358.

14   Guion, "Analysis of Selection Problems".

15   Ibid.

16   Ibid.

17   Frederick P. Morgeson, Kelly Delaney-Klinger, Melinda S. Mayfield, Phillip Ferrara, and Michael A. Campion, "Self-presentation Processes in Job Analysis: A Field Experiment Investigating Inflation in Abilities, Tasks, and Competencies," *Journal of Applied Psychology*, Vol. 89 (2004), 674-686; Jack E. Smith and Milton D. Hakel, "Convergence Among Data Sources, Response Bias, and Reliability and Validity of a Structured Job Analysis Questionnaire," *Personnel Psychology*, Vol. 32 (1979), 677-692; Suzanne Tsacoumis and Chad H. Van Iddekinge, "A Comparison of Incumbent and Analyst Ratings of O*NET Skills (FR05-66)," (Alexandria, VA: Human Resources Research Organization, 2006).

18   Brannick and Levine, "Job Analysis".

19   Ibid.

20   Dierdorff and Wilson, "A Meta-Analysis"; Tsacoumis and Van Iddekinge, "A Comparison".

21   Sanchez and Levine, "The Analysis of Work".

22   Filip Lievens, Juan I. Sanchez, and Wilfried De Corte, "Easing the Inferential Leap in Competency Modeling: The Effects of Task-Related Information and Subject Matter Expertise," *Personnel Psychology*, Vol. 57 (2004), 881-904.

23   Brannick and Levine, "Job Analysis"; Guion, "Analysis of Selection Problems"; Sackett and Laczo, "Job and Work Analysis".

24   Aguinis and Kraiger, "Benefits of Training and Development for Individuals and Teams, Organizations, and Society"; Sidney Gael, "Interviews, Questionnaires, and Checklists," in Sidney Gael, ed., *The Job Analysis Handbook for Business, Industry and Government* (New York: Wiley, 1988), Vol. 1, 391-414; Ernest J. McCormick and Paul R. Jeanneret, "Position Analyses Questionnaire (PAQ)", in S. Gael, ed., *The Job Analysis Handbook for Business, Industry and Government* (New York: Wiley, 1988), Vol. 2, 825-842.

25   Gael, "Interviews, Questionnaires, and Checklists"; M. D. Hakel, B. K. Stalder and D. M. Van De Voort, "Obtaining and Maintaining Acceptance of Job Analysis," in S. Gael, ed., *The Job Analysis Handbook for Business, Industry and Government* (New York: Wiley, 1988), Vol. 1, 329-338.

26   Cascio and Aguinis, "Applied Psychology".

27   Juan I. Sanchez and Edward L. Levine, "What Is (or Should Be) the Difference Between Competency Modeling and Traditional Job Analysis?" *Human Resource Management Review,* Vol. 19 (2009), 53-63.

28   Sanchez and Levine, "The Analysis of Work"; Jeffery S. Shippmann, Ronald A., Ash, Mariangela Batjtsta, Linda Carr, Lorraine D. Eyde, Beryl Hesketh, Jerry Kehoe, Kenneth Pearlman, Erich P. Prien, and Juan I. Sanchez, "The Practice of Competency Modeling," *Personnel Psychology,* Vol. 53 (2000), 703-740.

29   Sackett and Laczo, "Job and Work Analysis".

30   Sanchez and Levine, "The Analysis of Work".

31   Sackett and Laczo, "Job and Work Analysis".

32   Sanchez and Levine, "What Is (or Should Be)".

33   Lievens, Sanchez, and De Corte, "Easing the Inferential Leap".

34   Sackett and Laczo, "Job and Work Analysis"; Sanchez and Levine, "What Is (or Should Be)"; Shippmann *et al.*, "The Practice of Competency Modeling".

35   Sackett and Laczo, "Job and Work Analysis".

36   Sanchez and Levine, "What Is (or Should Be)".

37   Shippmann *et al.*, "The Practice of Competency Modeling".

38   Sackett and Laczo, "Job and Work Analysis".

39   Shippmann *et al.*, "The Practice of Competency Modeling".

40   Ibid.

41   Norman G. Peterson, Michael D. Mumford, Walter C. Borman, Edwin A. Fleishman, Kerry Y. Levin, *et al.* "Understanding Work Using the Occupational Information Network (O*NET): Implications for Practice and Research," *Personnel Psychology*, Vol. 54 (2001), 451-492.

42   Peterson *et al.*, "Understanding Work Using the Occupational Information Network".

43   Kenneth Pearlman, *Review and Analysis of Alternatives for a Common Service-wide Occupational Analysis System* (Washington, DC: U.S. Department of Defense, 2006); Roni Reiter-Palmon, Michael Brown, Darrel L. Sandall, CaraBeth Buboltz, and Thomas Nimps, "Development of an O*NET Web-based Job Analysis and its Implementation in the U.S. Navy: Lessons Learned," *Human Resource Management Review,* Vol. 16 (2006), 294-309; Teresa L. Russell, Andrea Sinclair, Jesse Erdheim, Michael Ingerick, Kimberly Owens, Norman Peterson, and Kenneth Pearlman, *Evaluating the O*NET Occupational Analysis System for Army Competency Development*, TR #1237 (Alexandria, VA: U.S. Army Research Institute for the Behavioral and Social Sciences, 2008).

44   Russell *et al.*, *Evaluating the O*NET.

45   Edward L. Levine, Francis Sistrunk, Kathryn J. McNutt, and Sidney Gael, "Exemplary Job Analysis Systems in Selected Organizations: A Description of Processes and Outcomes," *Journal of Business and Psychology*, Vol. 3 (1988), 3-21.

CHAPTER 2

MODELLING AND SIMULATION FOR MILITARY HUMAN RESOURCE PLANNING

STEPHEN OKAZAWA

Director General Military Personnel Research and Analysis
Department of National Defence, Canada

INTRODUCTION

This chapter discusses the application of modelling and simulation techniques to military human resources planning. The capability of a force to successfully carry out missions is, in large part, a product of the supporting HR system that recruits and develops the careers of military personnel. Therefore, the decision-making, policies and processes that shape the military HR system have a direct and significant impact on operations. However, understanding this system so that plans can be implemented that achieve desired outcomes is very challenging. Modelling and simulation are tools that can provide this understanding by predicting the outcomes of various options under consideration, thereby increasing confidence that planning objectives can and will be achieved through a chosen course of action.

Modelling and simulation are applied to military HR planning using the same approach as in other disciplines. A simulation is an experiment carried out using a model of a real system instead of the real system itself. For example, an experiment using a scale model of an aircraft in a wind tunnel is a simulation of the real aircraft in flight. This example illustrates several universal principles of modelling and simulation:

- The objective is to learn something about a complex system that is best determined by experimenting and observing the result. This means the information sought is neither obvious nor readily determined by theoretical analyses. For example, airflow over an aircraft and the resulting aerodynamic forces are a very complex system that is best studied by setting up experiments and taking specific measurements.

- The reason for using a model is that performing the experiment on the real system would either be impossible or too difficult and/or costly. Frequently, as in the example of wind tunnel testing, simulations are carried out before the real system is implemented in order to inform its final design by identifying potential problems and increasing confidence that it will function as planned.

- The model is a simplified version of the real system, therefore its behaviour will not be identical to the real system, but it will closely approximate the real system in ways that are important to the experiment. In the wind tunnel example, because the experimenters are interested in aerodynamic effects, the model aircraft accurately mimics the shape of the real aircraft, but the construction and internals of the model (e.g. Styrofoam and fibreglass) are as simple as possible and do not resemble the real aircraft. This is important as the model should not be more accurate or complex than it needs to be to gather the desired information. The cost-effectiveness and reliability of a simulation exercise diminish rapidly as the model's complexity increases.

- Simulation results can be used to infer certain properties of the real system, but only for those aspects of the model that are designed to approximate the real system. For example, it is possible to infer aerodynamic properties of the real aircraft by observing the model in the wind tunnel. But if the model aircraft broke apart at a certain wind speed, this would not imply anything about the real aircraft because the construction and strength of the model were not intended to approximate that of the real aircraft. Therefore, the limitations of the model should always be considered when interpreting simulation results.

In the domain of military HR planning, the real system is highly complex. It comprises the individual actions and decisions of all force personnel, a vast quantity of data pertaining to those individuals, and a bureaucracy that sets policy and manages those individuals. Problems that arise tend to have many causes that are difficult to identify, and the impacts of changes to the system are far reaching and manifest themselves over decades.

In order to make decisions with confidence that they will achieve planning objectives, it is necessary for military leadership to know as much as possible about the short and long term consequences of proceeding with various possible courses of action. Due to the complexity of military HR systems, these outcomes are very difficult to foresee. And because it is most likely infeasible to run experimental trials on the real HR system, simulation is often the best way of gaining the insights needed to make well-informed HR planning decisions.

In military HR simulation, computer software models of individual behaviour and military policy and processes are used. The models are typically populated with current data from the real HR system being studied. The models may be tuned so that their behaviour matches the historical behaviour of the real system. The options being considered by military leadership can be simulated in various scenarios that forecast what is likely to occur in the real system should that option be implemented. Scenarios are then compared using pre-determined measures that quantify the extent to which they achieve desired outcomes.

Sometimes, rather than simulating pre-determined scenarios for comparison, it is more effective for decision-makers to define which system parameters can be controlled and what are the limits on how much they can be adjusted. If this is done, an optimization procedure can be followed that uses simulation to search for the best-performing scenario by automatically varying the chosen parameters within acceptable ranges. In this approach, decision-makers focus on the desired outcome, allowing simulation techniques to produce recommendations on the best way to achieve it.

Many aspects of military HR systems are amenable to simulation as the necessary data exists and policies and processes involved are well defined and understood. Therefore, accurate models of HR systems can be developed, and reliable simulations can be carried out to gain information about probable outcomes given the current situation and available options. The following sections will describe several components of military HR systems for which modelling and simulation can play an important role in informing the planning process with examples and references drawn from research carried out at Defence Research and Development Canada.

TYPES OF MILITARY HR MODELS

Significant aspects of military HR systems that have a direct impact on the force's ability to conduct operations include recruitment, training, promotion, deployment and release. Not coincidentally, these are also major areas of military HR simulation.

Recruitment, promotion and release are typically simulated together using a class of model that will be termed a force structure model and are discussed as a unit. Training models will be discussed. Deployment falls into a broader class of model that will be termed a force employment model. In each case, the general structure of the model is presented as well as areas in which the simulation exercise can have a positive impact on HR planning. The data and information typically required to build the models are also described.

Note that the division of the HR system into these components for modelling purposes is artificial. In a real HR system, all the components interact with each other and with external factors. For example, if the training system is not able to keep pace with demand for specific courses and qualifications, the force's ability to generate qualified personnel for deployments and to promote individuals into higher ranks will be impeded. Thus, while a practical HR model will typically specialize in one area, it will often include simplified representations of other areas in order to account for some of these interactions.

FORCE STRUCTURE MODELS

A force structure model simulates the recruitment of individuals into the force, their promotion through the ranks, and their eventual release. These models simulate high level dynamics in the overall composition of the force. The objective of a force structure simulation is generally to determine whether recruitment numbers and promotion policies will be able to sustain a desired force structure given known release patterns.

Figure 2.1 shows the form of a typical force structure model. The force structure of an occupation is represented by a number of available positions in each rank. Recruits enter the occupation, usually at the lowest rank, occupying vacant positions. Promotions occur when an individual has met promotion requirements and a position is available in the next rank. Individuals may choose to release at any time from any rank based on specified release patterns. Specific applications may build on this basic structure in a number of ways. For example, multiple occupations may be simulated simultaneously with the possibility of cross-posting between occupations.[1] Frequently, detailed rules are required to determine when an individual becomes promotable and who will be selected for promotion when a position opens at a higher rank. Recruitment numbers may follow a specified intake plan, or they may dynamically respond to the demand for new recruits.[2] And in many cases, release rates are influenced by a number of factors tracked by the simulation including age, occupation, and years of service.[3]

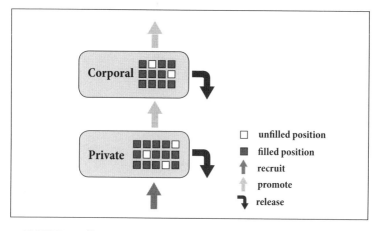

FIGURE 2.1: Illustration of a Force Structure Model Showing Recruitment, Promotion and Release

Impact

Force structure models can be used to answer a number of important questions in HR planning. Foremost among these, they can assess whether a desired force structure is achievable and sustainable. It is often not obvious that recruitment, promotion policy and release patterns may be at odds with a desired force structure. For example, an occupation might specify a manning level of 50 at the major rank, but if the pool of captains is not large enough, or if the time needed for captains to gain the experience required for promotion is too long, the major rank may be starved of incoming promotions. At the lieutenant-colonel rank, if the number of positions is too large or the time spent at that rank is too short, the major rank may be lose its experienced members as soon as they become promotable, again leaving vacant positions. Alternately, if the lieutenant-colonel positions are too few or the time spent in that rank is too long, promotion opportunities for majors will be rare and individual career progress may stagnate. These problems are structural and can occur even if recruitment and release rates are healthy. More generally, if release rates are low (often considered a good thing), new position openings will be infrequent, slowing the advancement of individuals through the ranks and causing an aging of the occupation, especially at higher ranks. Conversely if release rates are high or if many releases are concentrated at certain experience levels, position openings will occur frequently, encouraging the rapid promotion of individuals with less experience and potentially leaving the occupation below its preferred manning level for certain ranks. All these situations put strain on the HR system's ability to achieve or sustain a given force structure. Force structure simulation can help predict if these situations might arise in a given scenario, and the simulation results can be used to identify their cause and recommend corrective actions.

Force structure simulation can be particularly useful in evaluating the impact of proposed policy changes. For example, scenarios in which recruitment targets or promotion criteria are changed can be simulated and compared to the status quo. Two areas of policy that have a significant impact on force structure are terms of service and pensions. These factors have been found to be major driving forces behind release behaviour.[4] Releases tend to spike at the end of terms of service engagements and at important pension milestones, such as the point at which a pension can be collected without penalty. These release patterns determine the experience profile of the force (the number of individuals at each experience level measured by their accumulated years of service). Therefore, policy that affects release rates should be formulated such that the experience profile is inline with the desired force structure.[5] If the engagements and pension policy encourage members to release at experience levels that the force structure is in need of, or to stay at experience levels that are already saturated, then these policies are working against the operational requirements of the force that determine its force structure.

If a new force structure is proposed, simulation can be used to assess different scenarios of how the new structure can be achieved and the consequences of those differing approaches.[6] For example, the model might be used to simulate scenarios in which the force structure is grown by a certain amount over a period of three, five or ten years. In each of these scenarios, the required recruitment numbers and rate of advancement through the ranks (which has training and experience implications) can be determined. This can help assess the feasibility and cost of achieving a proposed force structure change in a given time frame.

In practice, force structure simulation has shown that rapid force growth or reduction introduces significant strains on the HR system and the consequences are felt for decades.[7] In these scenarios, recruitment rates are the most direct control point for growing or reducing a force. In a rapid growth scenario, the number of recruits must be drastically increased during the growth phase. This necessitates a similarly drastic increase in new recruit training capacity which has implications for cost and availability of training resources. Further, the growth in force numbers is not distributed throughout the force structure, but concentrated in a narrow experience band corresponding to the cohorts recruited during the growth phase. This unusually large number of individuals at roughly the same experience level will slowly move through the HR system over decades. Competition for career advancement within this group will be more intense, and career stagnation will be more likely. Because of its unusual size, releases from these cohorts will occur more frequently, and the vacancies will be difficult to fill from the smaller cohorts that followed the growth phase. This will be especially problematic when the growth cohort reaches retirement age. Similar problems occur as a result of rapid force reduction driven by drastic cuts to recruitment.[8] Therefore, it is generally advisable that force growth and reduction be implemented gradually and that attempts be made, where possible, to increase or reduce numbers at all experience levels corresponding to the needs of the desired force structure.

Inputs

The data requirements for basic force structure models are relatively straightforward. The model relies on planned intake data, historical release data, current population data and force structure data. Additionally, rules that specify promotion criteria and the prioritization of members eligible for promotions must be incorporated into the model. These inputs are mostly high-level data and information and are likely to be reasonably accurate and readily available. As a result, force structure simulations tend to be more straightforward to set up and produce reliable results with less effort than models that rely on more detailed data.

In practice, force structure models often include some basic aspects of training and force employment which add significantly to their complexity and data requirements.[9] These additions have the potential to increase model accuracy, but at the expense of reliability and simplicity. Their inclusion is, however, a logical progression once a basic force structure analysis has been completed.

TRAINING MODELS

Training models simulate the process of individuals attending training activities to acquire the experience and qualifications needed for career advancement and deployment. Training models simulate the supply of training capacity (e.g. trainers, equipment and facilities) and the demand among force members to receive the training. The objective of simulating a training system is, in general, to determine if training capacity is sufficient to meet demand.

Figure 2.2 shows the basic form of a training model that simulates training delivered in the form of a sequence of courses. These are frequently termed training pipelines. Each course has a capacity, duration and schedule. The schedule defines the dates on which individual classes for each course will begin. In the figure, individuals enter the pipeline at the start and determine which course they should attend. They are then registered for that course and wait in a queue for space to become available. If demand for the course is high, the wait time may be long. When they reach the head of the queue and a new class is scheduled to start, they are given a spot in that class. They attend the class for its duration. The model then determines if the student passed or failed. If they failed, the student returns to select another course or retake the same course. If they passed, qualifications associated with the completed training are granted. Then the model checks if the student has finished their training or if there are additional follow-on courses to take. In the latter case, the student returns to select the next course in the training pipeline. When all required courses are completed, the student exits the training system.

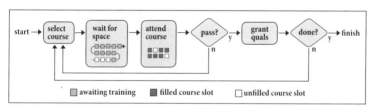

FIGURE 2.2: Illustration of a Training Model where Students Attend Scheduled Courses

In practice, there are many ways in which this simple model can be enhanced to deal with real scenarios. Occupation training is usually not linear as most training pipelines fork into multiple specialized streams. In these cases, the logic that determines the selection of students for different streams is included in the model.[10] For some types of training, especially those that rely on major equipment like simulators and ve-hicles, the training duration in the model may vary depending on the availability of the equipment and other factors like weather conditions.[11] The training activity may also take the form of what is often termed on-the-job training wherein there are no set classes or schedules. Instead, individuals gain practical experience over time at a rate determined by the number of trainers, the availability of equipment, and the number of other students.[12]

Impact

Fundamentally, training simulation can be used to determine wheth-er the production from a given training system meets the demand for qualified personnel. This is an important issue in the planning of basic training to ensure sufficient production of operationally qualified force members, and at higher ranks where career progression is tied to com-pletion of advanced courses. When HR planners are considering ac-tions that may change the demand for training, such as a change in force structure or a major new equipment acquisition, simulation can help determine the extent to which the training system will be able to meet the new production levels. If the training system is unable to keep pace with demand, then individual career progress will stagnate and the pool of personnel qualified for promotions, deployments and other activities will diminish, impacting the force's ability to conduct operations.

In addition to forecasting the production from a given training system with a specified capacity (number of courses, class schedules and class sizes), simulation can be used to determine the training capacity re-quired to meet a desired production level in a given time frame. For example, in planning the acquisition of new equipment, the arrival and phase-in of the equipment should ideally coincide with the completion of training of a sufficient number of personnel to use the new equip-ment. Simulation can be used to determine the training capacity needed to achieve this.

When a simulation indicates that the training system may not meet the demands placed on it in a given scenario, the results of the simulation can be analyzed to discover where the system broke down. There are many potential causes, the most straightforward of which are insufficient training capacity or an insufficient supply of personnel to the training system. Frequently, however, the problem is that many courses will have excess capacity but certain courses will be bottlenecks, running at full capacity with long wait times.[13] These situations are very inefficient for the training system as production for the whole pipeline is limited by a few bottlenecks, and downstream courses run with wasted extra space. Unused capacity is particularly problematic where training relies on major equipment and specialized trainers because their availability must often be planned far in advance. Simulation provides the ability to anticipate the demand for specific training activities over time in order to achieve desired production levels. If the planned supply of training capacity is less or more than necessary, then corrective action can be taken before problems arise.

Inputs

Typical training simulations require data on the current population of students along with any training qualifications they have attained so far, and they require information about the training system itself. This consists of planned training schedules, class capacities, durations, failure rates and qualifications awarded for all courses in the scenario. Further, the logic that determines the flow from one course to the next and the streaming into different career fields must be defined. This information is often not available in organizational databases and consists of a combination of hard rules, conventions, exceptions and case-by-case decisions applied by training managers. As a result, the subject matter expertise of training managers is typically an important input to the model building process. If the availability of trainers, facilities and/or equipment is an important consideration in planning the training system, then this information must also be provided.

These data requirements are generally quite involved and detailed. As a result, the accuracy of the data and the validity of the model and its output should be considered carefully.

FORCE EMPLOYMENT MODELS

Force employment models simulate the employment of force members on various activities over time. The main activities of interest are the elements of the readiness cycle, which are high-readiness training followed by deployment and then a waiver period. The latter of the three is a period of time during which force members returning from a deployment cannot be called upon to redeploy except under special circumstances and require that the force member waive the option to not deploy during this time. The objective of a force employment simulation is generally to assess the extent to which a force is able to generate and sustain a supply of qualified personnel that meets the demands of planned operations while respecting the readiness cycle.

Figure 2.3 shows the general form of a force employment model. The establishment consists of the personnel and organizational structure that make up the force being simulated. At a given time, a portion of the force members in the establishment will be available to begin a deployment. Others will be unavailable because they are already on high-readiness training, deployed, in the waiver period from a previous deployment or occupied for some other reason. Members selected to deploy must meet the requirements of the deployed positions defined for that activity. Once selected, members remain busy for the duration of the sequence of activities associated with the deployment and will be unavailable to participate in other deployed activities. Typical timings for these activities are six months for high-readiness training, six months on deployment, and twelve months for the waiver period. When the members complete the waiver period, they become available to deploy again.

There are many activities other than deployments that also occupy the time of force members. These include time taken for training, vacation, sick leave, injury, parental leave and others. These activities compete with deployments for the time of force members, though they can generally overlap with the waiver period following a deployment. In practice, force employment models typically incorporate non-deployed activities in some way; otherwise, the simulation may overestimate the number of force members available to deploy at a given time.[14] Additionally, the personnel selected for a given deployed activity are typically not drawn from all over the establishment, but are sourced from specific organizational units tasked to supply personnel to that activity.[15]

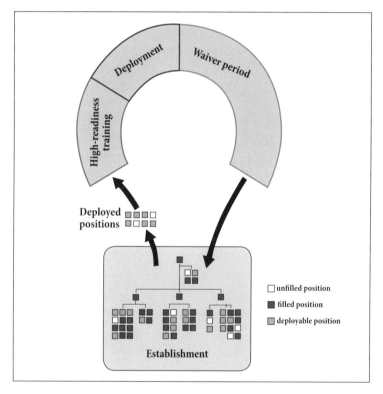

FIGURE 2.3: Illustration of a Force Employment Model Showing the Establishment Supplying Deployable Personnel to Activities Representing the Readiness Cycle

Impact

In general, force employment simulations can help assess the extent to which a force will be able to generate and sustain the supply of personnel for planned operations. This includes identifying which specific aspects of operations will be adequately supplied and which will experience shortages.[16] For those that are short, the simulation results can be analyzed to discover what specific issues led to the shortage. In many cases, the cause is that certain personnel with required qualifications were busy on other activities at the time they were needed. However, in some cases qualified personnel do exist, but the rules that determine which specific units are to supply a given deployed activity prevent their participation. In such cases, force employment simulation can also assist in planning the sourcing of personnel for planned operations.

Force employment simulation can also analyze the impact of conducting planned operations on the establishment. This includes forecasting which individuals, occupations and units will be in highest demand, and which will go largely unused.[17] These data can be used to assess the ability of a force to support intermittent surge operations as compared to baseline sustained operations. In the former case, various scenarios can be used to analyse the maximum magnitude and duration of surge operations that can be carried out before the supply of personnel is exhausted. The specific occupations and units that will begin to strain first and when this will likely occur can be identified. For sustained operations, it is possible to determine the maximum size and composition of a deployed force that can be supplied with ready personnel for an indefinite period.

The simulation of various force employment scenarios can also be used to assess the impact of changes to many aspects of force employment.[18] For example, the impact of changes to the number and type of parallel lines of operations that the force is planning to conduct can be investigated, and the impact of changes to the composition of a specific deployed force can be studied. Further, the relative duration of high-readiness training, deployments and the waiver period define the nominal ratio of the number of establishment positions required to sustain a single deployed position. Adjustments to these durations have a direct effect on the force's ability to support sustained operations. The impact of such changes can be quantified using force employment simulation.

Inputs

Force employment simulations require data on the deployed positions required for each activity being modeled, the scheduling and duration of those activities, and the personnel that make up the force establishment. If non-deployed activities are also to be included (such as time taken for training, illness, injury and leave) either explicit data or general information on how these events should be modelled must be provided. Frequently, all non-deployed activities are lumped into a single type of activity that periodically renders a certain percentage of the force non-deployable for a period of time.[19]

As with training models, this information is typically very detailed so the accuracy of the data and the validity of the model and simulation results should be carefully considered.

SUMMARY

This chapter introduced modelling and simulation in a military HR planning context. It defined models and simulations generally and described three important classes of military HR models in detail: force structure models, training models and force employment models. In each case, the general structure of the model was presented, and the impact its use can have on the HR planning process was emphasized.

However, the examples of military HR models described here should not be considered rigid. Each problem and each decision warrants its own approach and may call for a unique model of a specific aspect of the HR system. If the problem at hand is complex enough that first brush approaches (intuition, thought experiments and high-level calculations) are insufficient to confidently assess the outcome of potential courses of action, then a modelling and simulation approach should be seriously considered.

In general, making good planning decisions that have the highest chance of achieving desired outcomes is dependent on an accurate understanding of the system in which the chosen actions will be carried out. If this accuracy is lacking, actions taken will most likely be ineffective and may, in fact, be harmful. Because of its size and complexity, the behaviour of a military HR system and the short and long-term consequences of implementing possible courses of action are usually very difficult to foresee. However, a military HR system generally has well-defined structures and processes, and collects a large volume of data about itself. These qualities mean accurate computer models of many important aspects of an HR system can be built. Conducting simulation exercises using these models provides military planners with detailed knowledge of how the real HR system will likely respond in various scenarios. Ultimately, this enables military leadership to make decisions and provide direction in a complex environment with greater certainty that actions taken will effectively achieve planning objectives.

ENDNOTES

1   Stanley Isbrandt and Antony Zegers, "Arena Career Modeling Environment (ACME) Individual Training and Education (IT&E) Projection Tool," DRDC Technical Report TR 2006-03 (Centre for Operational Research and Analysis, Ottawa, Canada, 2006); Stephen Okazawa, Andrew Wind, and Antony Zegers, "Analysis of Proposed Changes to the Chaplain Occupations," DRDC Technical Memorandum TM 2005-12 (Center for Operational Research and Analysis, Ottawa, Canada, 2005)); Francois Larochelle, "Air Weapons System Technicians Excel Transition Model: User's Guide, 1st ed." DRDC Technical Memorandum TM 2010-030 (Director General Military Personnel Research and Analysis, Ottawa, Canada, 2010).

2   Antony Zegers and Stanley Isbrandt, "The Arena Career Modelling Environment – a New Workforce Modelling Tool for the Canadian Forces" Proceedings of the *2010 Summer Computer Simulation Conference*, Ottawa, Canada.

3   Stanley Isbrandt and Antony Zegers, "Artillery Non-Commissioned Member Occupation Group Modelling Projections: Career Progression and Individual Training and Education Projections," DRDC Technical Memorandum TM 2006-34 (Center for Operational Research and Analysis, Ottawa, Canada, 2006).

4   Nancy Otis and Michelle Straver, "Review of Attrition and Retention Research for the Canadian Forces," DRDC Technical Memorandum TM 2008-030 (Centre for Operational Research and Analysis, Ottawa, Canada, 2008).

5   Paul Bender and Leonard Kerzner, "Career Flow Implications of Terms of Service Proposals for Non-Commissioned Members," Project Report PR 2002-08 (Operational Research Division, Ottawa, Canada, 2002).

6   Larochelle, "Air Weapons System".

7   Isbrandt and Zegers, "Arena Career Modeling"; Bender and Kerzner, "Career Flow Implications" .

8   Bender and Kerzner, "Career Flow Implications".

9   Zegers and Isbrandt, "The Arena Career Modelling Environment".

10   Michelle Straver, Stephen Okazawa, and Antony Wind, "Training Pipeline Modelling Using the Production Management Tool," DRDC Technical Memorandum TM 2009-019 (Director General Military Personnel Research and Analysis, Ottawa, Canada, 2009).

11   Straver, Okazawa, and Wind, "Training Pipeline Modelling"; Rene Séguin, Chris Iverach-Brereton, and Jeremy Valcourt, "CFANS Air Navigator Resource

Allocation Model (ANAV-RAM) Simulation Tool: User's Guide and Technical Documentation," DRDC Technical Memorandum TM 2010-215 (Center for Operational Research and Analysis, Ottawa, Canada, 2010).

12   Ibid.

13   Straver, Okazawa, and Wind, "Training Pipeline Modelling"; Mike Ormrod, Stephen Okazawa, and Christine Scales, "Analysis of the Proposed Implementation of the New Army Communications and Information Systems Specialist (ACISS) Trade Using the Managed Readiness Simulator," DRDC Technical Memorandum TM 2011, in press, (Center for Operational Research and Analysis, Ottawa, Canada).

14   Patricia Moorhead, Andrew Wind, and Mira Halbrohr, "A Discrete Event Simulation Model for Examining Future Sustainability of Canadian Forces Operations," Proceedings of the *2008 Winter Simulation Conference*, S.J. Mason, R. Hill, L. Moench, and O. Rose, eds.; Chad Young, Raman Pall, and Mike Ormrod, "A Design Framework for Modelling Army Force Generation: Managed Readiness Simulator (MARS)," DRDC Technical Memorandum TM 2007-54 (Center for Operational Research and Analysis, Ottawa, Canada, 2007); Mike Ormrod and Chad Young, "Preliminary Analysis of Task Force Afghanistan Sustainability Using MARS," DRDC Technical Memorandum TM 2007-40 (Center for Operational Research and Analysis, Ottawa, Canada, 2007).

15   Ormrod and Young, "Preliminary Analysis of Task Force Afghanistan".

16   Ormrod and Young, "Preliminary Analysis of Task Force Afghanistan"; Patricia Moorhead and Mira Halbrohr, "An Operational Sustainability Model: A Tool for Examining Operational Sustainability from a Human Resources Perspective," DRDC Technical Memorandum TM 2010-104 (Center for Operational Research and Analysis, Ottawa, Canada, 2010) .

17   Mike Ormrod, Chad Young, and Raman Pall, "Modelling Force Generation with the Managed Readiness Simulator (MARS)," DRDC Technical Memorandum TM 2007-6 (Center for Operational Research and Analysis, Ottawa, Canada, 2007).

18   Moorhead and Halbrohr, "An Operational Sustainability Model"; Ormrod, Young, and Pall, "Modelling Force Generation".

19   Ormrod and Young, "Preliminary Analysis".

CHAPTER 3

SETTING DEPARTMENT OF DEFENSE RECRUIT QUALITY BENCHMARKS

JANE M. ARABIAN

Assistant Director, Enlistment Standards
Accession Policy Directorate
Office of the Under Secretary of Defense (Personnel & Readiness)
United States Department of Defense

BACKGROUND

Each year, the Military Services recruit approximately 200,000 men and women into the enlisted ranks. Qualification is based on numerous factors (e.g., age, citizenship, physical fitness, moral character), but key among these are educational attainment and aptitude. These latter two enlistment criteria are used to gauge recruit "quality," with a high-quality recruit defined as a high school diploma graduate who scores above average on the enlistment test. Determining how much quality is needed is a crucial issue when formulating enlistment policies and preparing recruiting budgets. Setting recruit quality benchmarks involves a trade-off between cost and performance. High-quality youth are more expensive to recruit than lower-quality youth, but they have lower attrition rates and they perform better both in training and on the job.

In 1985, Congress asked the Department of Defense (DoD) and the Services to define recruit quality requirements and to project those requirements over a five-year period. The resulting report, *Defense Manpower Quality*[1], provided estimates of the required percentages of recruits who

(a) were high school diploma graduates and (b) scored above average on the enlistment test. Estimates for the former ranged from 80 to 95 percent; estimates for the latter ranged from 59 to 68 percent. These estimates, however, were largely subjective (e.g., they were not tied to information about actual job performance). The department recommended at the time that the minimum quality benchmarks should be those observed in the recruiting population at large (which was 80 percent high school diploma graduates and 50 percent scoring above average on the enlistment test). Subsequently, the department sponsored several research projects aimed at gaining insight into identifying appropriate recruit quality requirements and obtaining the empirical data to set recruit quality benchmarks.

WHY QUALITY MATTERS

The department generally reports recruit quality along two dimensions – educational achievement and aptitude. Both are important, but for different reasons.

Education

We value recruits with a high school diploma because years of research and experience tell us that those with a high school diploma are more likely to complete their initial three years of service. About 80 percent of recruits with a high school diploma will complete their first three years, whereas only about half of those who failed to complete high school will make it. Those holding an alternative credential (e.g., General Educational Development (GED) certificate) fall between these extremes. (Table 3.1)

High School Diploma	80%
Other Credential (e.g., GED)	60%
Non-Graduates	50%

TABLE 3.1: How Many Candidates Complete Their First Enlistment

The better retention associated with those who complete high school saves money. In 1998, the General Accounting Office (GAO), now called the Government Accountability Office, provided an independent cost estimate of attrition.[2] In today's dollars, it would cost taxpayers upward of $50,000 to replace each individual who leaves service prematurely. This argues for recruitment of those who are most likely to adjust to the rigors of military life and stay the course. The high school diploma is a reliable indicator of such "adaptability."

Aptitude

Aptitude is a separate indicator of quality. All recruits take a written enlistment test called the Armed Services Vocational Aptitude Battery (ASVAB). One component of the ASVAB, the Armed Forces Qualification Test (AFQT), measures math and verbal skills. For reporting purposes, scores on the AFQT are divided into five categories: Cat I, 93-99; Cat II, 65-92; Cat III, 31-64; Cat IV, 10-20; and Cat V, 1-9 (ranges indicate percentile scores). Category III is often divided into subcategories IIIA (percentiles 50-64) and IIIB (percentiles 31-49). By law, applicants with AFQT scores below 31 (Cat IV and V) are ineligible to enlist, unless they are high school graduates.

Those who score at or above average on the AFQT are in Categories I-IIIA. We value these higher-aptitude recruits because their training and job performance are superior to those in the lower categories. Even with job experience, lower-aptitude enlistees show lower average job performance than do those with higher aptitude. For example, it takes three years for recruits scoring in Category IIIB to reach the average performance levels achieved within the first few months on the job by recruits scoring in Category I.

CHAPTER 3

THE COST-PERFORMANCE TRADEOFF MODEL

Higher-quality recruits (a) perform better, (b) stay longer, (c) are more expensive to recruit, but (d) are less expensive to retain than lower-quality recruits. How do the DoD and the Services decide how many high school graduates and people who score above average on the AFQT to enlist? The goal is to enlist a group of recruits so that the proportions of those with high school diplomas and those with above-average aptitude will be the least expensive group one could obtain that will perform to a desired level. The Accession Quality Cost-Performance Tradeoff Model (CPTM)[3] was developed to help set these quality benchmarks. The CPTM is based on two key linkages: (a) the relationship between recruit quality and job performance/attrition, and (b) the relationship between recruit quality and personnel costs.

Job Performance Information

The job performance information for the CPTM comes from the department's Job Performance Measurement (JPM) Project, a multi-million dollar effort that spanned 1980-1992.[4] The impetus for JPM was the discovery of a scoring error that inflated the ASVAB scores of lower-aptitude recruits. This miscalibration of ASVAB scores led to the enlistment of approximately 250,000 individuals who otherwise would not have qualified for entrance, and increased Congressional concerns about recruit quality.

As a response to the miscalibration, the DoD initiated the JPM Project. A primary goal of JPM was to determine if hands-on job performance could be measured. If so, then DoD could set enlistment standards on the basis of that job performance information (previous standards had been tied to training success rather than job performance). The JPM Project demonstrated that high-quality job performance measures could be developed, and that the relationship between a recruit's scores on the enlistment test and subsequent job performance was sufficiently strong to justify using the entrance test to set recruit quality benchmarks.

Technical Oversight by the National Academy of Sciences

Two committees of the National Academy of Sciences advised the DoD during the JPM Project. The Committee on the Performance of Military Personnel was formed in 1983 and provided technical oversight of research issues such as developing job performance measures and relating those measures to the enlistment test. Subsequently, the Committee on Military Enlistment Standards, chartered in 1989, provided technical oversight to development of the CPTM and its use in establishing recruit quality benchmarks.

THE CURRENT RECRUIT QUALITY BENCHMARKS

CPTM uses the relationships between job performance, recruit characteristics (e.g., aptitude, high school diploma graduate status), job characteristics (e.g., hands-on job tests, working in difficult conditions), attrition rates, and personnel costs to determine the number of recruits who will provide a desired level of job performance for the least cost. The costs in the CPTM are training costs, compensation costs, and recruiting costs (e.g., the number of recruiters and money for advertising, education benefits, and enlistment bonuses). Using these relationships, CPTM allows "what-if" analyses to examine how changes in one or more of these variables affect the other variables. For example, the department can investigate the predicted effect on recruit quality of scenarios such as:

- decreasing the advertising budget,
- decreasing the number of recruiters but increasing the advertising budget, and

- decreasing the money for enlistment bonuses and education benefits.

The purpose of the recruit quality benchmarks is to help ensure that recruit performance is sufficient to complete military missions. The CPTM cannot estimate how much quality is enough. The desired level of performance must be set by the policy-maker; it is a policy decision. However, CPTM can help identify the group of recruits that will provide the desired level of performance for the lowest cost.

What should be the desired performance level? The performance level specified by the policy analyst is a minimally acceptable value: "We need at least this much performance." For CPTM, the level of performance chosen was that provided by the 1990 recruit cohort, a group that provided satisfactory performance during Operations DESERT SHIELD and DESERT STORM. Specifying this level of desired performance resulted in the current recruit quality benchmarks that require 60 percent of recruits to have scores at or above average on the enlistment test (i.e., in Categories I-IIIA) and 90 percent to have high school diplomas.

The CPTM suggests that failure to achieve the recruit quality benchmarks would lead the department along a slippery track toward greater attrition and lower performance. Fortunately, the Services have exceeded these benchmarks since 1985 (see Figure 3.1). During 1990 (the baseline year), 68 percent of recruits scored in Categories I-IIIA and 93 percent had high school diplomas. This means that the Services were selecting their recruits in a nearly optimal, cost-effective manner given the desired level of job performance and goals for numbers of personnel across Service occupations.

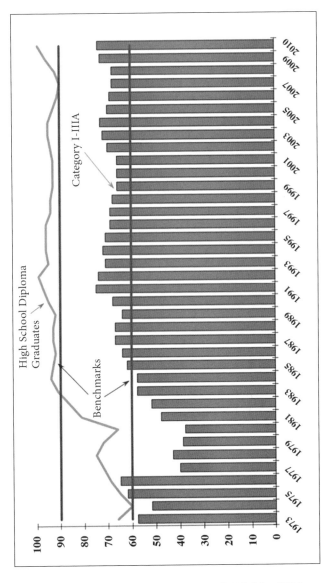

FIGURE 3.1: Percentage of Category I-IIIAs and High School Diploma Graduates from 1973-2010.

RE-EVALUATING THE RECRUIT QUALITY BENCHMARKS

The benchmarks identified by the CPTM reflect a minimal cost solution that depends upon the training, recruiting and compensation costs in the model. These costs, in turn, depend upon economic conditions. If the economy changes (e.g., the youth unemployment rate decreases), the costs in the model could also change (recruiting costs would increase), which in turn might lead to different benchmarks. Therefore, the benchmarks need to be monitored closely. Accordingly, the department re-evaluated the appropriateness of the current benchmarks in 2000.[5] This re-evaluation was especially important in the wake of the military drawdown and a robust economy. Also, additional job performance data became available after the CPTM was developed. These data were used to refine the relationship between recruit quality, recruiting resources, first-term attrition, and job performance. The result of the evaluation supported continued use of the initial benchmarks.

SUMMARY

The department has established recruit quality benchmarks of 60 percent who score at or above average on the enlistment test and 90 percent high school diploma graduates by examining the relationships between job performance, retention, and personnel costs, and establishing as its standard the performance level obtained by the reference cohort of 1990.

ENDNOTES

1   U.S. Department of Defense, *Defense Manpower Quality*. Report to the House and Senate Committees on Armed Services. (Washington, D.C.: Office of the Assistant Secretary of Defense (Manpower, Installations, and Logistics), 1985).

2   "Military Attrition: Better Data, Coupled with Policy Changes, could Help the Services Reduce Early Separations" (GAO/NSAID-98-213, September 1998).

3   B.F. Green Jr. and A.S. Mavor, Eds., *Modeling Cost and Performance for Military Enlistment*. Committee on Military Enlistment Standards, Commission on Behavioral and Social Sciences and Education, National Research Council. (Washington, D.C.: National Academy Press, 1994).

4   U.S. Department of Defense, *Joint-Services Efforts to Link Military Enlistment Standards to Job Performance*. Report to the House Committee on Appropriations. (Washington, D.C.: Office of the Assistant Secretary of Defense (Force Management and Personnel), 1992).

5   U.S. Department of Defense, *Review of Minimum Active Enlisted Recruit Quality Benchmarks: Do they Remain Valid?* Report to Congress. (Washington, D.C.: Office of the Assistant Secretary of Defense (Force Management Policy), March 2000).

CHAPTER 4

FINDING THE RIGHT PEOPLE: TAKING THE GUESSWORK OUT OF SELECTION

ANGELA VEARING and JENNIFER WHEELER
(formerly) Psychology Research and Technology Group
Canberra, Australia

MAJOR E. JAMES KEHOE, PhD
Australian Army Psychology Corps
Canberra, Australia

"You have too many warriors with you … Therefore, tell the people, 'Whoever is timid or afraid may … go home.'" So 22,000 of them went home, leaving only 10,000 who were willing to fight. The Lord told Gideon, "There are still too many! Take them down to the spring, and I will test them to determine who will go with you and who will not." So, Gideon took his warriors down to the spring to drink. The Lord told him, "Separate the men into two groups. In one group, put all those who cup water in their hands. In the other group, put all those who kneel down and drink with their mouths in the stream." Only 300 of the men drank from their hands. All the others got down on their knees and drank with their mouths in the stream. The Lord told Gideon, "With these 300 men I will … give you victory over the Midianites. Send all the others home." *Judges 7:2-7*

INTRODUCTION

Finding the right people for the right job is a crucial concern for organizations. For the Australian Defence Forces (ADF), finding the people who will succeed at training, on base, on operations, and, most importantly, in combat – land, sea, or air – is vital to executing military missions.

Beyond health and physical requirements, the intellectual, motivational, and emotional makeup of people has long been recognized as vital to their success or failure in an organization. In the military, testing for these qualities has been used since Biblical times, as described at the start of this chapter. Although the reasons are obscure, the warriors who stood up and drank from cupped hands were regarded by God as more battle-worthy than those who knelt to drink directly from the stream. From a modern perspective, this activity can be construed as a test of their situational awareness.

The aim of this article is to summarize the methods that are available for personnel selection. In addition to aptitude tests for specific abilities like languages, navigation, spatial orientation, and mechanical skills, these methods include:

- Tests of General Mental Ability (GMA);

- Interviews;

- Work sample tests;

- Tests of personality; and

- Assessment centres.

The following paragraphs will provide some discussion regarding each of these methods; however, before embarking on a discussion about different selection methods, it is important to understand validity.

VALIDITY: WHAT THE NUMBERS MEAN

Suppose there are 100 qualified applicants for a specific job, but only 25 are needed. The job is demanding and if all 100 applicants were accepted, only about half of them would perform satisfactorily. If 25 of the applicants were randomly accepted – perhaps by lottery or according to their application number – then about 12 or 13 would be successful. Thus, considerable time and effort in, say, training would be wasted on the remainder who failed. In addition, the failed personnel could have been usefully engaged elsewhere.

Method	Separate Validity*	Combined Validity
GMA tests	0.51	
Work sample tests	0.54	0.63
Interviews (structured)	0.51	0.63
Peer ratings	0.49	0.58
Job knowledge tests	0.48	0.58
T & E behavioural consistency	0.45	0.58
Job tryout procedure	0.44	0.58
Integrity tests	0.41	0.65
Interviews (unstructured)	0.38	0.55
Assessment centres	0.37	0.53
Biographical data measures	0.35	0.52
Conscientiousness tests	0.31	0.60
Reference checks	0.26	0.57
Job experience (years)	0.18	0.54
T & E point method	0.11	0.52
Years of education	0.10	0.52
Interests	0.10	0.52
Graphology	0.02	0.51
Age	-0.01	0.51

*The "Separate Validity" is the average validity coefficient for the method, and the "Combined Validity" is the average for each method when combined with GMA.

TABLE 4.1: Selection Methods and Their Predictive Validities for Job Success

How do we identify those applicants that can succeed? Here is where selection methods like those described in this article can and do help. The amount that a method can help is expressed mathematically by a statistic known as its *validity coefficient*. It ranges from 0 to 1. A test with a coefficient equal to 0 would provide no help whatsoever; guessing would work just as well. Conversely, a test with a coefficient equal to 1 would perfectly predict who would succeed and who would fail. No known method or set of methods has yet attained a validity of 1. At present, the best methods have coefficients around 0.50. In combination, the available methods can raise the validity to 0.65. Table 4.1 lists the known coefficients for a wide variety of tests alone and in combination with general mental ability.

What do these validity coefficients mean in practical terms? Consider a method – like work sample tests. Their validity is .54. If the 25 applicants with the highest work sample scores from a 100 applicants were selected for the job, then around 19 of them could be expected to perform well (76% success rate). When two tests with similar validities are combined, their joint validity increases. For example, GMA has a validity coefficient of .51. Together, work sample tests and GMA have a joint validity of .63. Using their results together would increase the success rate to 82% if the top quarter of applicants were selected. Thus, even tests with less than perfect validity can substantially increase the likelihood of selecting the right people.

The "Separate Validity" is the average validity coefficient for the method, and the "Combined Validity" is the average for each method when combined with GMA. Coefficients near 0.00 have little or no predictive value for job success. Higher coefficients, especially those above 0.40 have reasonable predictive value for job success, and a coefficient equal to 1.00 would be a perfect predictor. The following paragraphs will discuss different selection methods, including their relative validities.

GENERAL MENTAL ABILITY

GMA will be described more extensively in this book by Fogarty in Chapter 5. Across a wide range of organizations and jobs, tests of GMA help in predicting success in training and on the job. Nevertheless, GMA alone is hardly a perfect predictor and, for any particular job, GMA needs to be matched with the specific requirements of the job. We all know individuals who are bright enough but lack specific aptitudes and other qualities needed for success in some jobs. Recent research has revealed that the other methods listed can improve predicting who will be best suited for a job.[1]

INTERVIEWS

An interview is perhaps the method most commonly included in procedures for selecting applicants for training or a job. However, interviews are hardly all the same or equally useful. In addition to the specific content, interviews vary widely in their structure. At one extreme, there are interviews that have almost no structure; they are like ordinary conversations. Questions vary from applicant to applicant. In the middle is a range of semi-structured interviews – like selection boards – in which the questions are consistent across applicants, but their answers are evaluated in a qualitative way by the interviewers. Finally, there are highly structured interviews, in which the interviewers put exactly the same questions to all applicants, and the answers are scored according to a pre-determined rating scale.

Regardless of the structure of the interviews, the type of questions concerning job-related duties can include:

- *Past Behaviour*, e.g., "Tell us about a situation in which you had a subordinate who refused to …" and

- *Hypothetical Scenarios*, e.g., "How would you handle a subordinate who refused to ….?"

Superficially, these two types of questions appear equivalent. Each is intended to draw out the applicant's on-the-job problem-solving skills. Nevertheless, research has revealed that recall of past behaviour better predicts job performance than responses to hypothetical scenarios.[2] In fact, responses to hypothetical scenarios are weak predictors.

Structured interviews take time to develop. Moreover, they must be administered in a standardized format, which can be time consuming both in terms of training the interviewers and conducting the interviews. Nevertheless, the effort can pay off. For example, a study of health clinic managers found a solid correlation between interview score and supervisor-rated job performance.[3] When used in combination with GMA and personality factors, the results of structured interviews substantially improved their prediction of job performance (17%).[4] In contrast, a semi-structured interview only improved predictive accuracy by a small amount (4%), and an unstructured interview added very little (1%).

WORK SAMPLE TESTS

As the name implies, work sample tests are practical exercises in which the applicant performs a task that is closely related to the actual job or part of the actual job. These types of tasks include:

- *Hands On Tests.* The applicant performs the actual task. Tests of current competencies fall in this category;

- *Trainability and Aptitude Tests.* This method allows assessment of applicants who have no previous experience with the job. In some cases, applicants receive a certain amount of training on the task before being tested;

- *Situational Tests.* Rather than performing the task, applicants are given a scenario and then asked to describe how they would go about completing the task; and

- *Job Knowledge Tests.* These are usually tests that assess an applicant's knowledge about the job.

A major advantage of work sample tests is that applicants perceive the process as being fair. In addition, the tests allow the applicant to see what the job is like.[5] However, hands-on work sample tests are expensive to develop and administer, and most types can only be used with applicants who already have experience with the type of work. The increasing availability of high-fidelity simulations may make it more feasible to safely conduct hands-on tests with less experienced applicants.

PERSONALITY TESTS

The study of personality is what many people mistakenly think is the main type of psychological research. Nevertheless, personality testing does provide a worthwhile contribution to selection methods. A main advantage of personality tests is that they are relatively time-efficient to administer because a number of applicants can be assessed simultaneously. Potential disadvantages are that some questionnaires can be complex to deliver and time-consuming to score. Applicants may also fake answers to present themselves in a better light, although many modern tests have safeguards against such situations.

The five-factor model of personality explains that people can be described by a combination of five general dimensions of personality, including extraversion, emotional stability, agreeableness, conscientiousness, and openness to experience.[6] Among these, conscientiousness has been found to be the best predictor of overall job performance.[7] The aspects of job performance that are correlated with conscientiousness include citizenship behaviours, teamwork and job dedication. Conversely, a lack of conscientiousness predicts counter-productivity and organizational deviance. In the military context, emotional stability, when combined with GMA, is also a useful predictor of performance in training and on the job.[8]

ASSESSMENT CENTRES

Assessment centres are not a single method. Rather, they combine the main selection methods (e.g., aptitude tests, GMA, personality tests, work sample simulations, and interviews) into a single package that is given to a group of applicants over several days. Performance on these exercises is rated by a number of assessors, and ratings are integrated to provide an overall score. While the types of exercises used vary among assessment centres, they routinely use at least one simulation (e.g., one-on-one interactions, in-basket exercises, leaderless group discussions, and presentations).

An advantage of an assessment centre is that a number of applicants – usually 6-10 – can be assessed at the same time. The selection methods chosen for assessment centres are based on the results of a job analysis, so are therefore highly relevant to the particular job. Work sample simulations allow assessors to see dimensions of behaviour – such as behaviour in groups – that might not be possible to assess through other methods. Disadvantages of assessment centres are that they take considerable time to develop content, to train assessors, and to administer to the applicants.

The overall validity of assessment centres in general has not been clearly demonstrated in the research literature up to now. However, two recent studies have yielded promising results for predicting success in specific contexts. For Israeli police candidates, an assessment centre improved the prediction of training success (5%) and job performance (4%) above GMA.[9] Similarly, for German police candidates, an assessment centre performance explained 5% more variance in their job performance than GMA alone.[10]

OTHER METHODS

As can be seen in Table 4.1 (previously shown), a large number of other methods have been used for selection.[11] Some have proved worthwhile. Others, like graphology (handwriting analysis) have proven to be of little value.

Integrity Tests

Integrity tests are designed to predict counterproductive work-place behaviours. These tests typically present applicants with a hypothetical situation, and ask them to select the best alternative for how they would respond.

There are two main types of integrity tests.[12] First, Personality-Oriented Tests measure attitudes towards broader concepts, such as dependability, hostility, and social conformity. These tests tend to show correlations with the personality traits of conscientiousness, agreeableness, and emotional stability. Second, Overt Tests measure attitudes towards undesirable behaviours and also ask whether the applicant has engaged in this type of behaviour.

Integrity tests have relatively low development and administration costs, but applicants may fake answers in order to appear more socially desirable. Despite that risk, studies of their validity have continued to indicate that they do correlate with job success. In particular, personality-oriented tests are better predictors than overt tests.[13]

Peer Ratings

Peer ratings, as the name implies, ask co-workers or co-trainees to rate each other on job-related qualities. Peer ratings have generally poor overall validity. However, they may be more useful in specific contexts. In a recent study with Israeli police officers, peer ratings obtained during training correlated modestly with later supervisor ratings of job performance.[14]

Referee Reports

Referee reports are a common feature of selection procedures. Like interviews, they often entailed unstructured conversations or written reports. Like unstructured interviews, they have shown to be weak predictors of job success. However, a structured approach may be more useful. For example, 10-15 minute phone calls with referees using a 5-point scale to assess applicants' commitment/reliability, teamwork, and customer service have been found to moderately predict performance ratings by supervisors.[15]

Training and Job Experience

Measures of actual performance in training or performance on the job are good predictors of future job performance, although not as good as work sample tests.[16] In particular, the length of time in a job is not well correlated with future job performance.

CONCLUSIONS AND RECOMMENDATIONS

Anybody who has been involved in selecting an applicant for training or a job has probably thought that they were a good judge of an applicant's prospects for success or failure – that they could detect the unique merits or faults of an applicant. However, such decisions can be considerably improved by the use of standardized and validated tests of the applicants' knowledge, skills, attitudes, and abilities. Although no available method or combination of methods can yet entirely remove the guesswork from selection decisions, the methods themselves are constantly undergoing scrutiny and improvement, both inside and outside the ADF. Moreover, selection by the ADF does not rely on a single method but instead relies upon a spectrum of methods tailored to each occupation.

ENDNOTES

1   Frank L. Schmidt and John E. Hunter, "The Validity and Utility of Selection Methods in Personnel Psychology: Practical and Theoretical Implications of 85 Years of Research Findings," *Psychological Bulletin*, Vol. 124 (1998), 262-274.

2   Allen L. Huffcutt, Jeff A. Weekley, Willi H. Wiesner, Timothy G. Degroot, and Casey Jones, "Comparison of Situational and Behavior Description Interview Questions for Higher-level Positions", *Personnel Psychology*, Vol. 54, No. 3 (2001), 619-644; Henryk T. Krajewski, Richard D. Goffin, Julie M. McCarthy, Mitchell G., Rothstein, and Norman Johnston, "Comparing the Validity of Structured Interviews for Managerial-level Employees: Should We Look to the Past or Focus on the Future?" *Journal of Occupational and Organizational Psychology*, Vol. 79 (2006), 411-432.

3   Gedaliahu H. Harel, Anat Arditi-Vogel, and Tom Janz, "Comparing the Validity and Utility of Behavior Description Interview Versus Assessment Center Ratings," *Journal of Managerial Psychology*, Vol. 18 (2003), 94-104.

4   Jose M. Cortina, Nancy B. Goldstein, Stephanie C. Payne, H. Kristl Davison, and Stephen W. Gilliland, "The Incremental Validity of Interview Scores Over and Above Cognitive Ability and Conscientiousness Scores," *Personnel Psychology*, Vol. 53 (2000), 325-351.

5   Militza Callinan and Ivan T. Robertson, "Work Sample Testing," *International Journal of Selection and Assessment*, Vol. 8 (2000), 248-260.

6   Paul T. Costa and Robert R.McCrae. NEO PI-R Professional Manual. (Odessa, Florida: Psychological Assessment Resources, 1992).

7   Op cit.; Mitchell G. Rothstein and Richard D. Goffin, "The Use of Personality Measures in Personnel Selection: What Does Current Research Support?" *Human Resource Management Review*, Vol. 16 (2006), 155-180.

8   Jesus F. Salgado, "Big Five Personality Dimensions and Job Performance in Army and Civil Occupations: A European Perspective," *Human Performance*, Vol. 11 (1998), 271-288.

9   Kobi Dayan, Ronen Kasten, and Shaul Fox, "Entry-level Police Candidate Assessment Center: An Efficient Tool or a Hammer to Kill a Fly?" *Personnel Psychology*, Vol. 55 (2002), 827-849.

10   Diana E. Krause, Martin Kersting, Eric D. Heggestad, and George C. Thornton III, "Incremental Validity of Assessment Center Ratings Over Cognitive Ability Tests: A Study at the Executive Management Level," *International Journal of Selection and Assessment*, Vol. 14 (2006), 360-371.

11   Op. cit.

12   Christopher M. Berry, Paul R. Sackett, and Shelly Wiemann, "A Review of Recent Developments in Integrity Test Research," *Personnel Psychology*, Vol. 60 (2007), 271-301.

13   Deniz S. Ones, Chockalingam Viswesvaran, and Frank L. Schmidt, "Personality and Absenteeism: A Meta-analysis of Integrity Tests," *European Journal of Personality,* Vol. 17 (2003), 19-28.

14   Ronen Kasten and Kobi Dayan, "Relationship Between Peer Evaluations in a Police Academy and Various Measures of Future Police Performance," *Applied HRM Research*, Vol. 11 (2006), 119-122.

15   Paul J. Taylor, Karl Pajo, Gordon W. Cheung, and Paul Stringfield, "Dimensionality and Validity of a Structured Telephone Reference Check Procedure," *Personnel Psychology*, Vol. 57 (2004), 745-772.

16   Jennifer P. Bott, Daniel J. Svyantek, Scott A. Goodman, and David S. Bernal, "Expanding the Performance Domain: Who Says Nice Guys Finish Last?" *International Journal of Organizational Analysis,* Vol. 11 (2003), 137-152.

CHAPTER 5

INTELLIGENCE TESTING IN THE MILITARY: ORIGINS, USEFULNESS, AND FUTURE DIRECTIONS

MAJOR GERARD FOGARTY, PhD
Australian Defence Force

INTRODUCTION

Most, if not all, military systems in the modern world use some form of intelligence assessment to recruit the most suitable personnel and to place them in the right jobs. Intelligence assessment has also been a standard practice in private industry since the 1920s. Regarded as controversial at different times, the practice has been researched and debated extensively over the last 90 years. There is no shortage of material or topics to make the subject of an introductory chapter of this kind.

The present chapter is devoted to the origins of intelligence assessment in the military and to the fundamental question of whether or not intelligence assessment works. The chapter will close with a preview of some questions that should be addressed as we approach the second 100 years of intelligence assessment.

HISTORICAL ORIGINS OF INTELLIGENCE TESTING IN THE MILITARY

The word "intelligence" has ancient roots but one needs to go back no further than the early 1900s to find the origins of its modern usage. That's when Charles Spearman – an engineer and a retired British Army officer – was formulating his general factor theory of intelligence[1] and Alfred Binet was developing the first modern intelligence test, the Binet-Simon scale. These early steps were significant landmarks in the intelligence testing movement. Testing, however, was still conducted on an individual basis and not something that concerned the military.

That situation changed dramatically when the U.S. entered the First World War in 1917 and the army was confronted with the task of selecting and sorting almost two million inductees. A team of psychologists led by Colonel Robert Yerkes (as he preferred to be called) came up with three types of tests:

- the Army Alpha test for use with literate recruits;

- the Army Beta test for use with illiterate recruits; and

- an individual examination for those who failed the Beta test.

The Alpha version contained eight parts and used items that would be familiar to test-takers today. The Beta version used a pictorial format and contained items that, once again, would be found in many modern tests. Each recruit was graded from A+ to E- and suggestions for suitable army placement were made. Recruits scoring below C were considered unsuitable for officer training.

There were many problems associated with the content and administration of the Army Alpha and Army Beta tests and some strange results emerged. Stephen Jay Gould, the eloquent and acerbic critic of intelligence testing, took great pleasure in pointing out some of these oddities, such as the fact that the tests showed that the average mental age of white American adults was 13, which put them at the top of the "Moron" scale.[2] A second problem was that test administrators sometimes gave unclear instructions, the result that everyone in that particular test session came out with a score of zero.

It is easy to be critical of these initial attempts at intelligence testing in the military but one has to remember that most of the techniques were being trialled for the first time. In terms of content and administration, however, the Army Alpha and Army Beta tests laid the foundations for modern testing practices.

Once testing was established, it spread quickly to civilian life. Like other successful developments in science, misuses and abuses became all too common, making intelligence testing one of psychology's greatest achievements as well as one of its most controversial. Despite the misuses and the at times vehement criticism of intelligence testing, evidence continued to accumulate throughout the 20th century and into the 21st century that showed that testing technology had useful applications. In one of those quirks of history, we find that the first successful test of intelligence (Binet's) emerged at roughly the same time as the first tenable theory of intelligence (Spearman's), and both were able to capitalize on the newly developed statistical tool of correlation analysis (Francis Galton followed by Charles Spearman and Karl Pearson). The correlation techniques developed by these three pioneers – Galton, Spearman, and Pearson – not only provided a methodological tool for the further development of theories and tests of intelligence but also provided the means of showing that intelligence tests have predictive validity. That is, that they predict a reliable proportion of the variation one observes in real life performance.

A correlation coefficient is a statistic that estimates the degree of association between two variables. Values approaching +1.0 indicate a strong positive relationship. In other words, if you score highly on one variable, you tend to score highly on the other. Values approaching -1.0 indicate a strong negative relationship whereby a high score on one variable is associated with a low score on the other variable. Values around 0.0 suggest that there is no relationship between the two variables.

Whether or not intelligence tests predict real life performance is not a matter of opinion, it is a matter of empirical fact. In a testing context, the correlation is often referred to as a "validity coefficient". Thus, if we measure intelligence at one point in time and measure work performance at a later point, a significant positive correlation between the two variables is evidence of predictive validity. Furthermore, through a tool called "utility analysis", the correlation coefficient can also be entered into an equation that estimates the value of the test to the organization. The value increases as the validity coefficient increases.

INTELLIGENCE TESTS PREDICT WORK PERFORMANCE

Following Spearman, new theories of intelligence emerged and new tests were developed. There is not scope in this chapter to go into all these developments, but an important point is that despite various adjustments that had to be made to his theory, Spearman's notion of a general factor is still widely accepted today. We can call it "g", as Spearman did, a statistical abstraction representing the fact that tests of cognitive abilities are always correlated; or we can refer to it by its more usual name of GMA, the total score on a reasonably wide range of tests of mental ability, such as those comprising the selection test batteries of many military organizations around the world. GMA and g are not strictly equivalent but we will treat them as such here.

It was mentioned earlier that intelligence testing has always had its critics, fuelled by misuses of test results and unjustified extrapolations of findings. In the face of such criticism, one should expect to see strong evidence of correlations between GMA and work performance to justify the continued popularity of testing; and that is indeed what one does find.

In a special section of the 86th volume of the *Journal of Personality and Social Psychology* marking 100 years since the publication of Spearman's landmark paper on general intelligence,[3] was provided a succinct summary of the large body of research linking GMA with job performance. Conclusions were as follows:

- GMA predicts on-the-job performance to some extent in all jobs with correlations ranging from .20 in the simplest jobs to .80 in the most complex jobs;

- measures of GMA perform better than any other measure; and

- with the possible exception of conscientiousness/integrity, none of the less cognitive traits (e.g., values, interests) adds much, if anything, to the prediction of core job performance, except sometimes in narrow groups of jobs or when predicting peripheral aspects of job performance, such as organizational citizenship.

After such a strong general endorsement, one would expect testing within a military environment to show the same pattern. There are many hundreds of studies of the relationship between GMA and job performance, but almost all of this research is summarized by Schmidt and Hunter[4] and it leads overwhelmingly to the conclusion that GMA is a good predictor, and the best available predictor, of job performance, *including performance on military jobs.* The size of the validity coefficient varies according to the job family, but it is present for all jobs. Schmidt and Hunter also put to rest some other popular concerns about the relationship between GMA and job performance:

- The relationship is not restricted to test scores and training performance; it extends to the actual job situation. Thus, people who do better on the test tend to do better in training and then to maintain that advantage in the job itself. Ackerman's work on skill acquisition suggests that the mixture of abilities required for job performance changes over time as one acquires mastery of the task but these changes do not have appear to have a great impact on the importance of GMA.[5] One reason is that even though ability requirements may change over time, GMA is reflected to some extent in all cognitive abilities. A second reason is that in the modern work environment, many jobs do not settle into a steady pattern. They are constantly changing, imposing new demands for knowledge acquisition.

- There is no evidence in recent data that the relationship between GMA and job performance is decreasing. In fact, the reverse is likely to be true. Many researchers have commented on the increasing complexity of work situations.[6] What the research on GMA testing shows is that the correlation between test scores and job performance is higher with more complex jobs, so we can expect even higher validity coefficients in the future.

- Measures of personality traits, especially conscientiousness and integrity, add to the prediction of work performance but they are not as important as GMA.

WHY DOES GMA PREDICT JOB PERFORMANCE?

Schmidt and Hunter presented empirical data showing that GMA influences the ability to acquire knowledge and that better job knowledge mediates the effect of GMA on job performance.[7] In other words, people high on GMA learn tasks faster and better; they are faster to acquire both declarative and procedural knowledge, and that helps job performance.

HOW USEFUL IS INTELLIGENCE TESTING?

The practical value to the organization depends on the cost of training, the number of job applicants, variations in salaries and returns to the organization, and the size of the validity coefficient. Using a statistical tool called "utility analysis", it has been shown that for jobs that attract up to 20 applicants, a test with a validity coefficient of .6 can lead to a 100% gain in productivity.[8] The validity coefficients for many military jobs approach this range.

DO WE NEED TO CHANGE OUR TESTING PRACTICES?

This chapter has not explored the richness of the field of individual differences and the many other potential contributors to work performance, such as motivation. Nor has it reviewed the major developments in the field of intelligence over the past century. Instead, it has emphasized the point that much of what we learned about testing years ago still works today. In Cronbach's words: "Tests are like automobiles . . . the main working parts of today's machines were to be found in the cars of 1920 – society is slow to supplant an invention that works."[9]

However, as military folk know, when things are working well, complacency is a potential problem and some of the leaders in the field of testing are suggesting that we are entering into a state of complacency in relation to intelligence testing. Spearman's theory of general intelligence has long since been subsumed into more elaborate hierarchical models of intelligence but the concept of general mental ability is still embedded in those models, and measures of GMA can be obtained from modern test batteries because, by and large, item content and the structure of intelligence tests have not changed very much over the past 100 years.

By way of example, it has been claimed that the U.S. Armed Services Vocational Aptitude Battery, which is administered to over one million participants each year, is a state-of-the-art multiple aptitude test battery.[10] However, others have raised concerns about the ASVAB and have shown that it is basically a measure of crystallized intelligence (Gc), and therefore not the best collection of tests from which to extract a measure of GMA.[11] Others argue that the ASVAB should be revised to incorporate additional broad ability factors, particularly fluid intelligence (Gf) and learning and memory constructs. They were not concerned that the GMA drawn from the ASVAB has not served its purpose, rather they were concerned that human intelligence may be changing in response to technological and cultural evolution, while the tests remain unchanged.

Work demands change over time and cognition evolves to meet these new requirements. James R. Flynn was the first to draw attention to the gains in intellectual quotient (IQ) that are occurring with every generation.[12] But the so-called "Flynn Effect" is not due to an across-the-board increase in intellectual abilities. Vocabulary scores, for example, have not shown any gain. The gains are occurring in areas where educational and life experiences are posing challenges for successive generations.

What changes might we see in future intelligence test batteries? Perhaps an overemphasis on quantitative and verbal reasoning, and the relative lack of emphasis on spatial ability in current batteries.[13] It has also been argued that more emphasis on general fluid intelligence is required. We know from the various papers submitted by psychologists attending the *International Military Testing Association* conferences that questions concerning the currency of our intelligence test batteries are in the minds of most military organizations.

There is more to achievement than ability, much more. A validity coefficient ranging from .4 to .6 still leaves the larger portion of the variance in work performance unexplained. We must not become complacent about our testing achievements and should continue to monitor developments to ensure that validity coefficients do not decline over time and, equally important, to see if they can be improved. However, the onus of proof for the inclusion of new constructs must rest with their proponents. What research on the first 100 years of intelligence testing shows beyond reasonable doubt is that what we have been doing in the past has worked well.

As Hunt succinctly stated: "Psychometric tests do work".[14]

ENDNOTES

1   Charles Spearman, "General Intelligence Objectively Determined and Measured," *American Journal of Psychology*, Vol. 15 (1904), 201-293.

2   Stephen J. Gould, *The Mismeasure of Man*. (New York: Norton, 1981); Stephen J. Gould, "A Nation of Morons," *New Scientist*, Vol. 6 (May 1982), 349-352.

3   Linda S. Gottfredson, "Intelligence: Is It the Epidemiologists' Elusive 'Fundamental Cause' of Social Class Inequalities in Health?" *Journal of Personality and Social Psychology*, Vol. 86 (2004), 174-199.

4   Frank L. Schmidt and John Hunter, "General Mental Ability in the World of Work: Occupational Attainment and Job Performance," *Journal of Personality and Social Psychology*, Vol. 86 (2004), 162-173.

5   Phillip L. Ackerman, "Determinants of Individual Differences During Skill Acquisition: Cognitive Abilities and Information Processing," *Journal of Experimental Psychology: General*, Vol. 117 (1988), 288-318.

6   Earl B. Hunt, *Will We be Smart Enough? A Cognitive Analysis of the Coming Workforce* (New York: Russell Sage Foundation, 1995).

7   Schmidt and Hunter, "General Mental Ability".

8   Richard J. Herrnstein and Charles Murray, *The Bell Curve: Intelligence and Class Structure in American Life* (NY: Free Press, 1994), 84.

9   Lee J. Cronbach, *Essentials of Psychological Testing*, 4th ed. (New York: Harper & Row, 1984), 201.

10   Malcolm J. Ree and Thomas R. Carretta, "Group Differences in Aptitude Factor Structure on the ASVAB," *Educational and Psychological Measurement*, Vol. 55 (1995), 268-277.

11   Richard D. Roberts, Ginger N. Goff, Fadi Anjoul, Patrick C. Kyllonen, Gerry Pallier, and Lazar Stankov, "The Armed Services Vocational Aptitude Battery (ASVAB) Little More than Acculturated Learning (Gc)", *Learning and Individual Differences,* Vol. 12 (2000), 81-103.

12   James R. Flynn, "Massive IQ Gains in 14 Nations: What IQ Tests Really Measure," *Psychological Bulletin*, Vol. 101 (1987), 171-191; James R. Flynn, *What is Intelligence? Beyond the Flynn effect.* (Cambridge: Cambridge University Press, 2007).

13   David Lubinski, "Introduction to the Special Section on Cognitive Abilities: 100 Years after Spearman's (1904) "'General Intelligence,' Objectively Determined and Measured," *Journal of Personality and Social Psychology,* Vol. 86, No. 1 (2004), 96-111.

14   Hunt, *Will We be Smart Enough?,* 160.

CHAPTER 6

OCCUPATIONAL PERSONALITY: IMPLICATIONS FOR MILITARY ORGANIZATIONAL SETTINGS

ALLA SKOMOROVSKY, PhD

Director General Military Personnel Research and Analysis
Department of National Defence, Canada

"The outstanding characteristic of man is his individuality. There was never a person just like him and there never will be again."

Gordon Allport

INTRODUCTION

As stated in the previous chapter, most military systems in the modern world use some form of intelligence assessment to select applicants. Although not as common as intelligence testing, many military organizations also use occupational personality testing as a way to assess applicant's propensity to adapt to the rigors of military training and employment. This chapter is devoted to discussing the role of occupational personality in an organizational setting.

Occupational personality is concerned with individuals' fit in the work environment, their ability to work with others, and their performance potential against the job competencies. The goal of occupational personality is to apply the science of personality to the work environment in order to promote effectiveness and well-being of the individuals and the organization. In this chapter, the benefits of using a personality test for the military, the various strategies to assess personality, and their limitations, are discussed.

WHAT IS PERSONALITY?

Personality is defined as "consistent behaviour patterns and intrapersonal processes originating within the individual".[1] The first part of the definition concentrates on the consistency of one's behaviour across time and situations. This is important because it allows for predicting an individual's behaviour in the future. The second part of the definition concerns the "intrapersonal processes", – all emotional, motivational, and cognitive processes that can happen within an individual, affecting the way he or she behaves, feels, or thinks.

There have been six approaches that have attempted to explain the construct of personality. These approaches vary in the emphasis they put on individual differences in behaviours, emotions, and cognitions, in order to explain differences in personality. These approaches include the following:

a. psychoanalytical approach: focusing on the unconscious motives behind behaviours;

b. biological approach: focusing on the inherited predispositions and physiological processes;

c. humanistic approach: focusing on the feelings of personal responsibility and self-acceptance;

d. behavioural/social learning approach: focusing on conditioning, rewards/punishments, and expectations;

e. cognitive approach: focusing on the differences in the information processes and decision-making abilities; and

f. trait approach: focusing on the personality characteristics.

Although all six approaches provide important insights into the understanding of a person's personality, recently, most organizations focus on the trait approach. In fact, trait approach personality measures have been widely used in organizations for hiring and promotion decisions for many years.[2] The reason for this is that the trait approach is structured and measurable. Rather than relying on subjective judgements and complex concepts, the trait approach uses objective measures to examine the theoretical concepts. The trait approach is very useful in an organizational setting such as the military. Organizations should not expect any differences in the personality structure among males and females as well as across various languages and cultures.[3] Due to such an important role of the trait approach across areas, and in the industrial organizational sphere specifically, this paper concentrates on the trait approach to personality.

TRAIT APPROACH: FIVE FACTOR MODEL OF PERSONALITY

With the development of the Five Factor Model (FFM) of personality, the value of using the trait approach to personality has become widely accepted.[4] The factors of the FFM are most commonly labelled: conscientiousness, agreeableness, neuroticism, openness to experience, and extraversion.

Conscientiousness

Conscientiousness is related to the organizational domain of personality. Conscientious individuals possess such traits as motivation in goal-directed behaviour, persistence, dependability, conformity to rules, and attention to details.[5] These individuals are high achievers, dependable, persistent, capable of self-control and willing to take initiative – traits that positively influence group or organizational effectiveness and benefit the career of the individual. Conscientiousness is also a strong predictor of job satisfaction (over and above other personality traits and general cognitive ability).[6] Furthermore, conscientiousness can predict the effectiveness of a working team[7] and the overall performance in both civilian[8] and military jobs.[9] Therefore, military organizations should select individuals who obtain higher scores on conscientiousness.[10]

Agreeableness

Agreeableness is related to the moral domain of personality, given that it deals with the empathetic abilities of individuals.[11] Agreeable individuals possess such traits as being flexible, cooperative, tolerant, and being able to trust others. Agreeableness is an important personality trait for occupations involving teamwork[12] and leadership behaviours.[13]

Neuroticism

Neuroticism is related to the emotional domain of personality. This trait is comprised of two dimensions: anxiety (instability and stress proneness) and overall mental health (the feeling of insecurity and depression).[14] Individuals high in neuroticism may be prone to anxiety, hostility, depression, anger, self-consciousness, vulnerability, insecurity, and impulsiveness, while individuals low in neuroticism regularly adjust better to stressors.[15] In addition, individuals high in neuroticism are more likely to be dissatisfied with their jobs (disregarding the type of the job).[16]

Emotionally stable individuals perform better at their jobs. Indeed, individuals low in neuroticism were found to perform better at their jobs,[17]and under stress, individuals high in neuroticism are less able to cope effectively and, thus, are more prone to develop depression.[18] Therefore, high stress occupations, such as the military, should select individuals who are low in neuroticism (i.e., emotionally stable).[19]

Openness to New Experiences

Openness to new experiences is related to the intellectual domain of personality. Individuals who are open to new experiences possess such traits as imagination, curiosity, broad-mindedness, creativity, and intellectual interest. Due to their motivation and ability to learn, these individuals would perform better at their jobs[20] and training.[21] Furthermore, openness to new experiences is an important personality trait for leaders.[22] Thus, openness is important for occupations when training and leadership behaviours are involved.

Extraversion

Extraversion is a social domain of personality and is described as a need for stimulation. Extravert individuals are sociable, energetic, talkative, assertive, and outgoing. Individuals high in extraversion regularly experience more positive emotions than those low in extraversion[23] and are more resilient to developing depression under stress.[24] In addition, given that individuals who are high in extraversion are more communication-orientated and sociable, extraversion is an important trait for leaders.[25] Therefore, organizations should select individuals who are higher in extraversion, especially for occupations involving teamwork and leadership behaviours.

To conclude, personality is an important predictor of job performance, as well as for individual's mental health. Individuals high in extraversion, agreeableness and conscientiousness as well as low in neuroticism have better psychological well-being.[26] For example, individuals high in neuroticism are more prone to depression, anxiety, and self-blame; experience more physical illness and psychological distress. Those high in extraversion are more likely to use social support to cope with life stressors. Therefore, in order to maximize job performance, ensure good psychological well-being, and job satisfaction, hiring decisions should take individual's personality into account. Military organizations should select individuals who are high in conscientiousness, extraversion, openness to new experiences, and agreeableness, and low in neuroticism.

In the CF, the need for psychological screening has already been recognized. Personality measures are currently used to select personnel for tactical teams and crews (e.g., snipers),[27] and are being considered for use to all CF personnel. Personality measures have been shown to be good predictors of:

- success in basic officer and recruit training;[28]

- psychological well-being of personnel; and

- general life and training satisfaction.[29]

TRAIT-SELF DESCRIPTIVE PERSONALITY INVENTORY

Personality can be assessed in an interview or in a self-report personality inventory. Organizations find that the self-report assessment is a more cost-efficient method, as the testing can be administered to several people at a time and the administration requires less time and supervision. One of the most common self-report measures of the FFM of personality is the Trait-Self Descriptive Personality Inventory (TSD-PI). TSD-PI was originally developed for the United States Air Force (USAF) to facilitate the selection of Air Force personnel.[30] Multiple research studies by the Australian Defence Force, the CF, and the USAF have demonstrated that this inventory is a valid and reliable measure of personality.[31] Research conducted in the United Kingdom has demonstrated that the TSD-PI was related to performance and leadership potential. With regard to the prediction of military performance, agreeableness, openness to experience, and neuroticism predicted military officer training performance in the U.S., particularly interpersonal skills such as leadership.[32] In Canada, conscientiousness, neuroticism, and extraversion, measured by the TSD-PI, predicted non-commissioned member (NCM) and officer cadet performance during Basic Recruit Training (BRT) and Basic Officer Training Course (BOTC) better than other personality measures investigated. This research resulted in a recommendation to employ the TSD-PI as the preferred personality measure for use in CF selection.[33]

SELF-REPORT APPROACH TO ASSESS PERSONALITY: PROBLEMS AND LIMITATIONS

Despite the number of benefits associated with the use of personality testing for selection purposes, there is a concern that faking may occur. The self-report method to assess personality depends on the participants' ability and willingness to provide accurate information about themselves.[34] In the industrial organizational setting, faking is a serious concern, because the test-takers would be motivated to present themselves in a favourable light. These individuals would fake their scores, trying to present themselves in a more positive way than they actually are.

In personnel selection, when there is a strong incentive to make a positive impression in order to get a job, faking would be an important consideration. Indeed, even moderate faking was found to be strongly and negatively affect selection decisions and reduce the usefulness of the test.[35] If individuals are selected into an organization based on their fake scores, their performance on the training and the job may not be satisfactory.[36] The FFM of personality, and especially the conscientiousness and neuroticism domains, were found to be susceptible to faking.[37]

One of the ways to reduce faking is to advise applicants against faking. Thus, providing a warning about the inclusion of a faking scale in a personality test would benefit the selection system as it might diminish the amount of faking.[38]

Other researchers have proposed including an actual impression management scale to identify individuals who fake.[39] Such a measure would examine an individual's general tendency to present the self in a more context desirable manner. If faking is identified, there are several options to consider:

- disregard the personality scores of an individual who faked;

- adjust the score for each individual; and

- correct the personality scores for the social desirability index.

The first approach of taking an individual out of competition when faking is supected is not recommended, especially when there is a high demand for applicants. Adjusting a score for each individual (e.g., during an extensive interview process) becomes problematic when a large number of applicants are involved. Finally, the automatic correction can be calculated by subtracting a certain predetermined number from the person's score. For example, those who fake, automatically have 10 points deducted from their total score. This procedure was found to result in positive changes in the hiring decisions.[40] Researchers have suggested that the automatic correction is the most useful method from a practical perspective. Although there is some criticism for using an impression management (IM) scale to minimize the effects of faking,[41] it remains the best strategy to counter the effects of the potential faking in an effort to restore the validity of the personality scale.[42]

CONCLUSION

There is consistent evidence suggesting the usefulness of a personality test in organizational settings. Results of multiple studies presented in this chapter demonstrate that taking an individual's personality into account for selection or promotion decision will optimize important personnel decisions. Individuals who are psychologically fit for the job will perform better in training and on the job, will be more likely to be satisfied with the job and stay in the organization, and will have better psychological well-being. Although personality assessment has its limitations, such as impression management behaviour, there are ways to decrease and counter its negative effect. Overall, organizations striving to maximize individuals' job performance, ensure their psychological well-being, and reduce attrition, should select individuals who are high in conscientiousness, agreeableness, openness to new experiences, and extraversion, as well as low in neuroticism.

ENDNOTES

1   Jerry M. Burger, *Personality*. 6ᵗʰ ed., (Thomson Learning Inc. USA, 2004).

2   Robert T. Hogan, "Personality and Personality Measurement", in Marvin D. Dunnette and Leaetta M. Hough, eds., *Handbook of Industrial and Organizational Psychology*, Vol. 2, 2nd ed., (Palo Alto, CA: Consulting Psychologists Press, 1991), 873-919.

3   Robert R. McCrae and Paul T. Costa Jr., "Personality Trait Structure as a Human Universal," *American Psychologist*, Vol. 52 (1997), 509-516; Paul T. Costa Jr., Robert R. McCrae, and D.A. Dye, "Facet Scales for Agreeableness and Conscientiousness: A Revision of the NEO Personality Inventory," *Personality and Individual Differences,* Vol. 12 (1991), 887-898.

4   Murray R. Barrick, Michael K. Mount, and Timothy A. Judge, "Personality and Job Performance at the Beginning of the New Millennium: What Do We Know and

Where Do We Go Next?" *International Journal of Selection and Assessment*, Vol. 9 (2001), 9-30.

5   Thomas S. Bateman and J. Michael Crant, "The Proactive Component of Organizational Behaviour" *Journal of Organizational Behavior*, Vol. 14 (1993), 103-118.

6   Timothy A. Judge, Chad A. Higgins, Carl J. Thoresen, and Muray R. Barrick, "The Big Five Personality Traits, General Mental Ability, and Career Success Across the Life Span," *Personnel Psychology*, Vol. 52 (1999), 621-652.

7   Jill Kickul and George Neuman, "Emergent Leadership Behaviours: The Function of Personality and Cognitive Ability in Determining Teamwork Performance and KSAs," *Journal of Business and Psychology*, Vol. 15 (2000), 27-51.

8   Murray R. Barrick and Michael K. Mount, "The Big Five Personality Dimensions and Job Performance: A Meta-analysis." *Personnel Psychology*, Vol. 44, (1991), 1-26.

9   Jeffrey J. McHenry, Leaetta M. Hough, Jody L. Toquam, Mary Ann Hanson, and Steven Ashworth, "Project A Validity Results: The Relationship Between Predictor and Criterion Domains," *Personnel Psychology*, Vol. 43 (1990), 335-354; Timothy A. Judge, Joseph J. Martocchio, and Carl J. Thoresen, "Five-factor Model of Personality and Employee Absence," *Journal of Applied Psychology*, Vol. 82 (1997), 745-755.

10   Judge, Martocchio, and Thoresen, "Five-factor Model".

11   Bateman and Crant, "The Proactive Component".

12   Judge, Martocchio, and Thoresen, "Five-factor model".

13   Timothy A. Judge and Joyce E. Bono, "Five-factor Model of Personality and Transformational Leadership," *Journal of Applied Psychology*, Vol. 85 (2000), 751-765.

14   Paul T. Costa, Jr. and Robert R. McCrae, *Revised NEO Personality Inventory and Five Factor Model Inventory Professional Manual* (Odessa, FL: Psychological Assessment Resources, 1992).

15   Bateman and Crant, "The Proactive Component".

16   Judge, Martocchio, and Thoresen, "Five-factor Model".

17   Kickul and Neuman, "Emergent Leadership Behaviours"; Jesus F. Saldago, "The Five Factor Model of Personality and Job Performance in the European Community," *Journal of Applied Psychology*, Vol. 82 (1997), 30-43.

18   Alla Skomorovsky, E. Nisbet, R. Westmacott, K. Matheson, and H. Anisman, "Stress and Depression: The Role of Personality, Self-Esteem and Coping," Paper

presented at the *Annual Convention of the Canadian Psychological Association,* NL, 2004.

19   Stanley L. Crawford and Edna R. Fiedler, "Development and Current Status of USAF Mental Health Screening," *Military Medicine*, Vol. 156, No. 11 (1991), 596-599.

20   Judge, Martocchio, and Thoresen, "Five-factor Model".

21   Barrick and Mount, "The Big Five Personality Dimensions".

22   Barrick and Mount, "The Big Five Personality Dimensions".

23   David Watson and Lee Anna Clark, "Extraversion and its Positive Emotional Core," in R. Hogan, J. Johnson, and S. Briggs, eds., *Handbook of Personality Psychology* (San Diego, CA: Academic Press, 1997), 767-793).

24   Skomorovsky *et al.*, "Stress and Depression".

25   Kickul and Neuman, "Emergent Leadership Behaviours"; Judge and Bono; Watson and Clark; Mary H. McCaulley, "The Myers-Briggs Type Indicator and Leadership," in Kenneth E. Clark and Miriam B. Clark, eds., *Measures of Leadership* (West Orange, NJ: Leadership Library of America, 1990), 381-417.

26   Robert R. McCrae and Paul T. Costa, Jr. "Adding Liebe and Arbeit: The Full Five-factor Model and Well-being," *Personality and Social Psychology Bulletin*, Vol. 17 (1991), 227-232; Keith Magnus, Ed Diener, Frank Fujita, and William Pavot, "Extraversion and Neuroticism as Predictors of Objective Life Events: A Longitudinal Analysis," *Journal of Personality and Social Psychology*, Vol. 65 (1993), 1046-1053.

27   David Scholtz and Marcel Girard, "The Development of a Psychological Screening Program for Sniper Selection," Technical Note 2004-05 (Director Human Resources Research and Evaluation, Department of National Defence, Ottawa, Ontario, Canada, 2004).

28   Damian O'Keefe, "Development of an Optimal Trait-Self Descriptive Inventory (T-SD) Profile for Military Police Applicants," Technical Note 99-2 (Director Human Resources Research and Evaluation, Department of National Defence, Ottawa, Ontario, Canada, 1999).

29   Alla Skomorovsky, "Psychological Well-Being and Alcohol Consumption of Canadian Forces Recruits: The Role of Personality and Gender," Technical Memorandum., In press. (DRDC CORA, 2008).

30   Raymond E. Christal, Jerry M. Barucky, Walter E. Driskill, and J.M. Collis, "The Air Force Self Description Inventory (AFSDI): A Summary of Continuing Research,"

Draft Technical Report CDRL A004 (Armstrong Laboratories, Brooks AFB, USA, 1997).

31   J.M. Collis and C.C. Elshaw, *The Development of the Trait-Self Description Inventory, Results of US/UK Collaboration, TTCP/HUM/98-001, The Technical Cooperation Program: Military Human Resource Issues* (Technical Panel HUM-TP3, Human Assessment Laboratory, UK, 1998); F. Syed and J.D. Klammer, *The Trait-Self Description (TSD) Inventory: An Examination of the Issues, TTCP/HUM/02/03, Technical Panel HUM-TP3*, Military Human Resources Issues, The Technical Cooperation Program(2002).

32   Christal *et al.*, "The Air Force Self Description".

33   Damian O'Keefe, "Investigating the Use of Occupational Personality Measures in the Canadian Forces Selection System," Technical Note 98-14 (Director Human Resources Research and Evaluation, Department of National Defence, Ottawa, Ontario, Canada, 1998).

34   Burger, *Personality*.

35   N.T. Nguyen and M.A. McDaniel, "Faking and Forced-Choice Scales in Applicant Screening: A Meta-Analysis," Paper presented at the annual meeting of the *Society for Industrial and Organizational Psychology,* New Orleans, LA, 2000.

36   Michael L. Zickar *et al.*, "Modeling the effects of faking on personality tests," Paper presented at the *11th Annual Meeting of the Society for Industrial and Organizational Psychology,* San Diego, CA, 1996; Joseph G. Rosse, Mary D. Stecher, Janice L. Miller, and Robert A. Levin, "The Impact of Response Distortion on Preemployment Personality Testing and Hiring Decisions," *Journal of Applied Psychology*, Vol. 83 (1998), 634-644.

37   Neil D. Christiansen, Richard D. Goffin, Norman G. Johnston, and Mitchell G. Rothstein, "Correcting the 16PF for Faking: Effects on Criterion Related Validity and Individual Hiring Decisions," *Personnel Psychology,* Vol. 47 (1994), 847-860.

38   Stephen A. Dwight and John J. Donovan, "Do Warnings Not to Fake Actually Reduce Faking?" *Human Performance*, Vol. 16 (2003), 1-23; Jennifer Wheeler, L.S. Hamill, and N.T. Tippins, 'Warnings against candidate misrepresentations: Do They Work?" Paper presented at the Eleventh Annual Conference of the Society for Industrial and Organizational Psychology, San Diego, CA, 1996; Lynn A. Mcfarland, "Warning Against Faking on a Personality Test: Effects on Applicant Reactions and Personality Test Scores," *International Journal of Selection and Assessment*, Vol. 11 (2003), 265-275.

39   J.F. Edens *et al.*, "Effects of Positive Impression Management on the Psycho-pathic Personality Inventory," *Law and Human Behavior*, Vol. 25 (2001), 235-256.

40   Christiansen *et al.*, "Correcting the 16PF for Faking" Linda Hough, "Effects of Intentional Distortion in Personality Measurement and Evaluation of Suggested Palliatives," *Human Performance*, Vol. 11 (1998), 209-244.

41   Deniz S. Ones, Chockalingam Viswesvaran, and Angelika D. Reiss, "Role of Social Desirability in Personality Testing for Personnel Selection: A Red Herring," *Journal of Applied Psychology*, Vol. 81 (1996), 660-679.

41   Christiansen *et al.*, "Correcting the 16PF for Faking".

CHAPTER 7

THE ASSESSMENT CENTRE METHOD: ORIGINS, VALUE AND BEST PRACTICES FOR PERSONNEL SELECTION

ANGELA VEARING and JENNIFER WHEELER
(formerly) Psychology Research and Technology Group
Canberra, Australia

INTRODUCTION

The assessment centre technique in personnel selection has been increasing in use and acceptance in organizations and government agencies. Assessment centres are also a method employed by the military for the selection of personnel for discrete military occupations, including officer, aircrew, and special forces entry. An assessment centre is a personnel selection method that incorporates multiple selection tools (e.g. group tasks, job simulations, oral presentations) that are given to a group of applicants usually over one to two days. Applicants' performances on a number of exercises are assessed by multiple trained assessors.[1]

The objective of an assessment centre is to value-add to the personnel selection continuum, by allowing the observation of traits that might not be measured by other selection methods such as intelligence testing or interviews. The format of an assessment centre allows an applicant's interaction and influence in a group environment to be observed and assessed, thereby demonstrating personal qualities such as leadership and oral communication. Other job specific knowledge and skills can also be assessed through job simulation tasks.

Since assessment centres are expensive and time-consuming to develop, administer and maintain, it is important to determine whether they predict job performance over and above less expensive personnel selection measures, such as cognitive ability tests and interviews. In other words, do assessment centres provide enough unique information that can justify the extra time and money? The focus of the present chapter is to provide an overview of the assessment centre approach and its use in personnel selection. This will include a brief history of assessment centres, a description of the characteristics of a good assessment centre, and research demonstrating the value of assessment centres in predicting job performance. The chapter will conclude by considering the future of assessment centres for personnel selection.

HISTORICAL ORIGINS OF ASSESSMENT CENTRES

The first assessment centres were developed in Germany after the First World War, with the aim of selecting military officers.[2] These assessment centres were mainly focused on measuring leadership potential through the use of paper-and-pencil tests, behavioural observation, handwriting analysis, and job simulations.

During the Second World War, the assessment centre technique was adopted by the British army for the selection of officers, and was called the War Office Selection Board (WOSB). Its introduction was largely motivated by the "drop in the supply of good material" from private schools in Britain.[3] The WOSB provided a solution to the recruiting crisis and introduced an objective and scientific way to assess officer applicants from a variety of educational classes. In 1954, Australia introduced a modified version of the WOSB in order to select officer applicants for the army, and this process is still in place today.

Today, the assessment centre method is employed in a number of nations for military selection. Its primary use is in the selection of personnel for specialized military roles, or for occupations with expensive or intensive training programs. Outside of the military, the assessment centre technique is used widely to select applicants for a number of different types of organizations, such as government, law enforcement, and educational institutions.[4]

DEFINITION OF AN ASSESSMENT CENTRE

An assessment centre is a technique used to select applicants for a particular job, and usually involves at least one day of exercises such as role plays and presentations. The exercises are designed to assess behaviours that have been classified into specific dimensions, and performance is rated by a number of trained assessors.

The *Guidelines and Ethical Considerations for Assessment Centre Operations*,[5] specify that for an assessment method to be called an "assessment centre", it must contain:

a. multiple assessors;

b. multiple assessment exercises (at least one must be a simulation);

c. multiple behavioural dimensions to assess; and

d. integration of ratings made by assessors.

CRITERIA FOR A GOOD ASSESSMENT CENTRE

Several criteria have been identified as essential for conducting an effective assessment centre.[6]

They include:

- a job analysis;
- defined dimensions;
- good exercises;
- qualified assessment;
- applicant preparation; and
- good behaviour documenting and scoring.

Job Analysis

A job analysis must be conducted on the specific position for which the assessment centre will be selecting applicants. A job analysis utilizes subject matter expert advice to determine the essential attributes required for successful performance in a job. This will ensure that the assessment centre tests applicants on criteria that are relevant to the job.

Defined Dimensions

Once the job analysis has been conducted, each essential attribute should be classified into a specific dimension of behaviour. Dimensions must describe behaviour that is observable. Assessment centres with fewer dimensions have been found to predict job performance better than those with many dimensions.[7] This is probably because there are fewer demands placed on assessors to observe the different types of behaviour, thereby leading to more accurate ratings.

Good Exercises

Exercises must then be chosen that will allow assessors to observe the behaviours defined in the dimensions. These exercises must resemble the actual job, but be general enough to not unfairly advantage applicants who might already be employed within the organization. Exercises must also be standardized, so that each applicant is presented with the same situation. Simulations are an essential component of assessment centres, and may include one-on-one interactions, in-basket exercises, leaderless group discussions, and oral presentations. Table 7.1 provides a description of each type of simulation, the dimensions of behaviour it can be used to measure, and the relative advantages and disadvantages of each.[8]

Simulation Exercise	Description	Examples	Dimensions	Advantages	Disadvantages
One-On-One Interactions	This is usually a role play with a trained person, and involves a situation that is related to the job.	Dealing with a difficult customer	- oral communication - persuasiveness - leadership ability - listening skills - problem solving	- realistic - job-specific - quick to administer	- time consuming to prepare situation and train role players - difficult to keep situation consistent for each applicant
In-Basket Exercises	This exercise is where applicants are given a situation where a number of tasks are required to be completed.	Responding to phone messages, e-mails and letters	- decision-making - directing others - organization - following instructions	- realistic - job-specific	- difficult to develop - time-consuming to administer and score - possible adverse impact on minority groups
Leaderless Group Discussions	This activity is where applicants are given a situation with a problem, and asked to work together in a group to develop a solution.	Developing a new policy, building a tower	- leadership - interpersonal communication - motivation - flexibility - problem solving	- easy to score - a number of applicants can be assessed at the same time	- difficult to standardize situation (different applicants in each exercise)
Oral Presentations	This exercise is where the applicant is asked to give an oral presentation on a given topic.	Presenting a review of an article	- oral communication - stress tolerance - imagination	- easy to score	- can only assess each applicant separately

TABLE 7.1: Types of Simulation Exercises Used in Assessment Centres

Qualified Assessors

Assessors should be trained prior to being involved in an assessment centre. Specifically, they should be trained to understand the dimensions and exercises, techniques for observing and rating behaviour, and how to provide feedback. Assessors should also be familiar with the job being applied for.

Applicant Preparation

It is advised that applicants are informed about the process of the assessment centre, such as the objectives, who the assessors are, what information will be collected, how the results will be stored, and the type of feedback given. This information is necessary to ensure that applicants are adequately informed about the assessment centre, which will increase the standardization between applicants and reduce measurement error.

Good Behaviour Documenting and Scoring

For an assessment centre to be effective, behaviour rating must be objective and accurate. An effective rating scale would be behaviourally anchored, which ensures that all raters understand the meaning of each score. An example of a good rating scale is a 6-point scale as follows:[9]

- 5 = A great deal of the dimension was shown (excellent).

- 4 = Quite a lot of the dimension was shown.

- 3 = A moderate amount of the dimension was shown (average).

- 2 = Only a small amount of the dimension was shown.

- 1 = Very little was shown, or this dimension was not shown at all (poor).

- 0 = No opportunity existed for this dimension to be shown.

HOW WELL DO ASSESSMENT CENTRES PREDICT TRAINING AND JOB PERFORMANCE?

To determine the extent to which assessment centre results predict subsequent job and training performance, researchers calculate the strength of the relationship between the variables. This relationship is called a correlation coefficient, and ranges from 0 to 1. Further information on correlation coefficients can be found in an earlier chapter on intelligence testing.

A review of personnel selection studies conducted over the past 85 years found the assessment centre method to be predictive of subsequent job performance (correlation coefficient of .37).[10] Since this review, a number of recent studies have continued to find evidence that assessment centres predict future aspects of job performance. For example, a study on health care managers in Israel found that assessment centre performance was significantly correlated with performance assessments made by supervisors.[11] Another study demonstrated that assessment centre ratings predicted perceptions of fitting into the organization for graduates in Ireland.[12] Recent research also found that assessment centre performance predicted success for political candidates in the United Kingdom.[13] Assessment centres have also been found to predict other criteria, such as later job performance, training success, and promotions; however, they did not predict future turnover.[14] Where predictive validity was established, the correlations remained significant even when the criterion (e.g., job performance) was measured 5 to 10 years after the assessment centre was conducted. The correlations were also relatively equal among the employment groups studied (business, military/police, and schools). These studies show strong support for the value of assessment centres in personnel selection.

DO ASSESSMENT CENTRES PREDICT JOB PERFORMANCE OVER AND ABOVE OTHER MEASURES?

While many studies have provided evidence that assessment centres are able to predict job performance, there is little research regarding whether they predict over and above other less expensive measures, such as cognitive ability tests. In other words, it would not be worthwhile to spend time and money developing an assessment centre, if it does not predict job success any better than a cognitive ability test would. In a review of personnel selection research, Schmidt and Hunter reported that assessment centres did not predict job performance over and above cognitive ability.[15] The authors suggested that this result may be attributable to the strong relationship between the two variables, as the majority of studies used in the review included a cognitive ability test as part of the assessment centre.

Since the Schmidt and Hunter review, two recent studies provide evidence of the value of assessment centres over and above cognitive ability.[16] Both studies examined police force candidates, and measured cognitive ability and assessment centre performance separately. The first used a sample of candidates for the Israeli police force.[17] In this study, candidates were first given cognitive ability tests. Those who achieved a satisfactory score on the tests then took part in a two-day assessment centre. The study found that both cognitive ability scores and assessment centre ratings predicted final training score and later job performance. Additionally, assessment centres provided a unique contribution over and above cognitive ability, explaining an additional 5% of the variance in final training scores and 3.9% of the variance in supervisor ratings of job performance.

The second study was conducted with executive-level police officers in Germany.[18] This research found that cognitive ability and assessment centres were both correlated with training outcomes (i.e., final exam grades) after 2 years. In addition, assessment centres explained an extra 5% of the variance in training performance over and above the cognitive ability test. The authors concluded that assessment centres provided value over and above a measure of cognitive ability.

FUTURE DIRECTIONS FOR ASSESSMENT CENTRES

The future of assessment centres will most likely be linked to advances in technology. It has been suggested that technological advances will change the types of exercises that could be included in assessment centres.[19] For example, simulation exercises might be presented on a computer to represent current office requirements. In fact, a whole office environment could be set up to simulate more realistic in-basket activities, which could involve interaction with e-mail, telephones, and filing systems. Presentation of exercises via computer programs could also reduce the time and costs associated with scoring.

THE VALUE OF THE ASSESSMENT CENTRE METHOD

The research presented in this chapter has generally found assessment centres to be good predictors of later job performance and training success. While there is mixed evidence for their value over and above cognitive ability tests, assessment centres may be able to provide qualitative information to the assessor regarding desirable attributes for job performance. For example, the assessor is able to see how an applicant performs when giving a presentation, and can see first-hand how they interact with others in group activities. In the military, assessment centres can provide information on essential attributes such as leadership, oral communication, teamwork skills, and personal qualities.

An assessment centre may therefore be able to provide information that a cognitive ability test or interview alone may not show; specifically behavioural observations and measures of job performance. The assessment centre method can enhance the accuracy of selection decisions through increasing the scope and nature of information on each applicant. This method may also reduce potential limitations between an applicant's verbal description of their abilities (e.g. during an interview) and actual work behaviour. As illustrated:

> Most of us can cite personal examples in which we know the correct way of doing something, like hitting a backhand shot in tennis, tuning the motor of a car, or organizing our work and study habits more efficiently, yet do not translate that knowledge well into work behaviours.[20]

Organizations will need to weigh the costs of developing and maintaining an assessment centre against the value potentially gained through an increased range of applicant information. This cost-benefit decision will most likely depend upon the particular attributes required for the occupation, whether these attributes require assessment through an interactive, observational and/or group selection technique and the nature and intensity of the subsequent training/job role.

ENDNOTES

1   Dennis A. Joiner, "Guidelines and Ethical Considerations for Assessment Center Operations: International Task Force on Assessment Center Guidelines," *Public Personnel Management*, Vol. 39 (2000), 315-331.

2   Tim J. Newton, "Discourse and Agency: The Example of Personnel Psychology and 'Assessment Centres'," *Organization Studies*, Vol. 15 (1994), 879-903.

3   Newton, "Discourse and Agency", 886.

4   Joiner, "Guidelines and Ethical Considerations".

5   Ibid.

6   C. Caldwell, George C. Thornton III, and M. Gruys, "Ten Classic Assessment Center Errors: Challenges to Selection Validity," *Public Personnel Management*, Vol. 32 (2003), 73-88.

7   C. M. Hardison and P. R. Sackett, "Assessment Center Criterion Related Validity: A Meta-analytic Update," Paper presented at the *18th Annual Conference of the Society for Industrial and Organizational Psychology*, Chicago, U.S., April 2004.

8   George C. Thornton III and Deborah E. Rupp, "Simulations and Assessment Centers", *Comprehensive Handbook of Psychological Assessment: Industrial and Organizational Assessment*, Vol. 4, (2004), 319-344; Harry Tolley and Robert Wood, *How to Succeed at an Assessment Centre*, 2nd ed. (Great Britain: Kogan Page Ltd., 2006); Kenneth M. York, David S. Strubler, and Elaine M. Smith, "A Comparison of Two Methods for Scoring an In-basket Exercise," *Public Personnel Management,* Vol. 34 (2005), 271-281.

9   Robert D. Gatewood, Hubert S. Field, and Murray Barrick, *Human Resource Selection*, 6th ed. (Australia: South-Western Thomson Learning, 2008), 628.

10   Frank L. Schmidt and John E. Hunter, "The Validity and Utility of Selection Methods in Personnel Psychology: Practical and Theoretical Implications of 85 years of Research Findings," *Psychological Bulletin*, Vol. 124 (1998), 262-274.

11   Gedaliahu H. Harel, Anat Arditi-Vogel, and Tom Janz, "Comparing the Validity and Utility of Behavior Description Interview Versus Assessment Center Ratings," *Journal of Managerial Psychology*, Vol. 18 (2003), 94-104.

12   Thomas N. Garavan, "Using Assessment Centre Performance to Predict Subjective Person-organisation (P-O) Fit: A Longitudinal Study of Graduates," *Journal of Managerial Psychology*, Vol. 22 (2007), 150-167.

13   Jo Silvester and Christina Dykes, "Selecting Political Candidates: A Longitu-dinal Study of Assessment Centre Performance and Political Success in the 2005 UK General Election," *Journal of Occupational and Organizational Psychology,* Vol. 80 (2007), 11-25.

14   Hardison and Sackett, "Assessment Center Criterion Related Validity".

15   Schmidt and Hunter, "The Validity and Utility of Selection Methods".

16   Ibid.

17   Kobi Dayan, Ronen Kasten, and Shaul Fox, "Entry-level Police Candidate As-sessment Center: An Efficient Tool or a Hammer to Kill a Fly?" *Personnel Psychology,* Vol. 55 (2002), 827-849.

18   Diana E. Krause, Martin Kersting, Eric D. Heggestad, and George C.Thornton III, "Incremental Validity of Assessment Center Ratings Over Cognitive Ability Tests: A Study at the Executive Management Level," *International Journal of Selection and Assessment*, Vol. 14 (2006), 360-371.

19   George C. Thornton III and Deborah E. Rupp, *Assessment Centres in Human Resource Management: Strategies for Prediction, Diagnosis, and Development* (USA: Lawrence Erlbaum Associates, Inc., 2006).

20   Robert D. Gatewood and Hubert S. Feild, *Human Resource Selection*, 5th ed. (Australia: South-Western Thomson Learning, 2008), 633.

CHAPTER 8

ONLINE TESTING:
CHALLENGES AND PROMISE

MELINDA HINTON and JAMIE SWANN
Australian Department of Defence

"SEEK" AND YOU SHALL FIND

The introduction of the World Wide Web (WWW) in 1992, and the development of internet browsers, such as Netscape in 1994, has provided the general public access to an interactive information volume that is unprecedented. In an increasingly competitive job market, organizations across the globe have merged this expanding technology into their recruitment strategies to gain the edge on applicant attraction. Defence organizations have also made use of the expansive reach of internet recruitment, with all nations within the TTCP having well-established and comprehensive recruitment websites (see Table 8.1). These websites comprise job and organizational information, selection processes and requirements, and multimedia attraction techniques (e.g. pictures, videos, military-style games) to whet the appetite of potential recruits. Many have taken a further step, allowing applicants to initiate their application process online (e.g., online career guidance, initial application of biographical and *curriculum vitae* information).

EXAMPLES OF DEFENCE RECRUITMENT WEBSITES:

Australia: http://www.defencejobs.gov.au/

Canada: http://www.navy.forces.gc.ca/cms_careers/careers-home_e.asp

New Zealand: http://www.stepup.mil.nz/

UK: http://pathfinder.armyjobs.mod.uk/

US: http://www.goarmy.com/

TABLE 8.1: TTCP Nation Military Recruiting Websites

For any organization, the advantage of internet recruitment is threefold:

- the standard time from job-posting to hire is significantly decreased;

- internet recruitment is economical, showing significant cost savings comparative to traditional methods; and

- the ability of job candidates to view vacancies and submit applications via the internet results in larger candidate pools per job.[1]

BIGGER IS NOT ALWAYS BETTER

"...the ability to attract larger candidate pools [via internet recruitment strategies] does not equate to attracting a higher proportion of quality candidates"
(Lawrence, 1999; cited in Bartram 2000).[2]

The opportunities provided by internet recruitment also bring their own unique challenges. Larger applicant pools, generated from broader accessibility, place significant pressure on an organization's selection processes (the system used for sifting suitable applicants). Incorporation of psychological assessment (e.g. cognitive ability, situational judgement, and personality tests) to improve the validity of job selection decisions, combined with the need for efficient applicant sifting, has prompted calls for similar technology to that being used for attraction and recruitment, specifically the internet, to be used for test delivery. This shift in delivery method could include using remote testing to pre-sift applicant pools, reducing the number of applicants invited for face-to-face testing and interviewing.

The potential for psychological tests to be delivered via the internet prompted reviews by both the American Psychological Association (APA) and International Test Commission (ITC) resulting in a comprehensive review of Internet-Based Testing issues[3] (IBT) and best-practice guidelines for IBT administration.[4] The four primary issues raised by these reviews were:

- the technological feasibility of administering a psychological test on the internet;

- the security of the test and personal information of the applicant;

- the type of test, its purpose, and the preservation of its reliability and validity; and

- test-taker authenticity and identification of cheating.

However, before these issues can be discussed in more detail, some preliminary definitions must be established.

DEFINING THE TECHNOLOGY

There are three technological solutions to administering a test via a computer. These are:

- computer-based testing;

- intranet-based testing; and

- internet-based testing.

Computer-based Testing (CBT)

CBT Refers to any psychological test that is delivered via a stand-alone computer. The advantages of CBT administration of psychological tests include: efficient and accurate recording of responses; immediate and automatic scoring; and savings on expendable material needed for more traditional test methods (e.g., pencil-and-paper).

Intranet-based Testing (INBT)

The test is delivered on a computer which is linked to a central server, with availability to multiple users, via a closed access network. INBT provides advantages over CBT, including: test results are available immediately to the organization, regardless of location; and updates of instructions, test items, scoring techniques and normative distributions can be made from a central location and are active immediately.

Internet-based Testing (IBT)

The test is delivered on a computer with network access, with testing available via the WWW or equivalent public access server. IBT takes the advantages of INBT a step further. With remote access for test-takers, IBT allows wider accessibility and added convenience for applicants with internet access. Furthermore, the costs and resource time involved in establishing and maintaining an IBT system may be less than those involved in running recruiting centres, computer-based or otherwise.

DEFINING THE TEST TYPE AND PURPOSE

In determining the feasibility of using the internet for psychological test administration, the ITC Guidelines identify that the purpose of testing is a primary consideration.[5] Test purpose can be broadly categorized as being either low or high stakes tests.

Low Stakes Tests

Low stakes tests are, typically, for the benefit of the applicant to assist career/job choice. These may comprise self-report inventories to assist person-job/organization fit or cognitive ability testing as an indicator of jobs the applicant is potentially suitable for.

High Stakes Tests

High stakes tests are, typically, for the benefit of the organization to screen in the best applicants, or screen out applicants who may present a training/job risk. These tests may comprise cognitive abilities assessment, personality inventories, bio-data and or situational judgement tasks.

Both the type of test (cognitive or non-cognitive) and the test purpose may govern the suitability of administration via the internet.[6]

DEFINING THE ADMINISTRATION MODE

The ITC Guidelines have proposed four basic *modes* of administration for psychological testing: Open; Controlled; Supervised; and Managed.[7] These modes (see Table 8.2) provide an increasing degree of identification, standardization and security, and may be viewed as appropriate depending on the test purpose.

ITC Modes of Administration

Open Mode. No supervision of test administration and the test-taker can access the test via the internet without registration.

Controlled Mode. No supervision of test administration, however the test-taker is known and must be provided with a login and password to access the test.

Supervised Mode. Test-taker accesses the test under supervision at an unsecured location (e.g. a school or local library). Qualified administrator begins and closes the test.

Managed Mode. Test-taker accesses the test under supervision at a secure location. Qualified administrator begins and closes the test.

TABLE 8.2: ITC Modes of Test Administration

101

THE CHALLENGES OF IBT

Despite the promise of easier and cheaper applicant selection and filtering, there are distinct technical, psychological, ethical and administrative challenges that can severely reduce the utility of IBT. The following five conditions will need to be met if organizations are to take advantage of IBT.

Challenge 1: It Must be Technologically Feasible

There are specific technical considerations for an organization embarking on IBT. In reviewing the possible transfer of the Computer Adaptive Testing-Armed Services Vocational Aptitude Battery (CAT-ASVAB) to internet delivery, researchers have identified 5 specific differences in technology of IBT, compared with CBT:[8]

- *Equipment ownership*. The ownership of the hardware used for testing is highly variable, and typically owned by the test-taker, thus IBT must be, within reason, hardware independent.

- *Graphical user interface*. IBT must be designed to suit modern internet applications.

- *Response input medium*. Responding to the test must be conducted via commonly owned peripherals (e.g. mouse, keyboard).

- *Testing control software*. Test administration software cannot be platform-specific, and must have broad compatibility.

- *Data storage location*. Data is not isolated to a single location or computer, thus data storage is required to be remote and transferred via the internet between secured (or unsecured) servers.

In addition to these technical differences, IBT introduces a higher requirement for technical control and support. This includes hardware (local and remote access servers), network (internet service provision and bandwidth) and human resources (programming capability, help desk support) requirements.

Challenge 2: It Must be Secure

When considering IBT, the test user must provide security to protect for threats both to test integrity and intellectual property, and to the confidentiality of the test-takers' personal, or "in-confidence" information.[9] Two primary security issues must be managed: data storage and security while "in transit",[10] and security of the test items and scoring when remotely accessed.[11]

The permanent storage of test items, execute files, scoring keys and respondent information must be maintained at a high level of security, protecting the information from unauthorized access and dissemination. Secure storage options must be available at the test user's site, via (potentially) a fire-walled proxy and independent test database which separates the information from the broader internet. To deliver the information to the respondent, without creating delays due to internet access or bandwidth, test users may consider downloading an erasable execute file onto the respondents Random Access Memory (RAM), where the file is deleted on completion of the test or shut-down of the computer. Software development has provision for data encryption which may ensure security of the data in transit. While encryption does not necessarily prevent interception, it does ensure that the data itself is unable to be read or used by an external party. The advent of modern encryption technology has been evidenced by the success of internet banking worldwide.

Ensuring the security of the test items while in use is a more complex issue. Even though the test items may be stored remotely on a server, they will be displayed on a test-taker's computer during administration, which leaves items open to being copied. While some measures, such as disabling computer functions (e.g. "Print screen" or "Copy/Paste") or password-limited single-use access can protect items; there is little protection from having an interested party simply write the items down during testing or take a picture. In the case of high-stakes testing, the uncontrolled distribution of test items can significantly compromise the utility of the selection system.

One promising solution to increased test security is Computer Adaptive Testing (CAT). CAT presents the applicant with a minimal number of items from a larger pool, with item selection governed by applicant ability. As such, any one applicant is not exposed to, nor has the opportunity to replicate, all items available, and each individual receives a unique variant of the test.[12] However, as yet, there is no method that completely secures a test from illegal access if presented in an open or controlled mode of administration.

Challenge 3: It Must Discourage and Detect Cheaters

It is difficult to envisage any alternative, at present, to the need for an accountable and responsible other person to be present during any assessment where issues of authentication and control over cheating matter[13]

Establishing test-taker authenticity is relevant to all modes of administration; however, it is more difficult in the Open and Controlled modes as the test-taker is accessing the test unsupervised. The issues raised in establishing test-taker authenticity may also apply to identifying "cheaters" who may be using contraband aids (calculators, pen and paper, rulers, dictionaries or books) against test instructions, or gaining assistance from another person to complete the test.[14] IBT also opens the possibility of an applicant using a computer (look-up dictionaries/thesauri, software calculators, etc.) or internet resources to aid their performance in a test.[15]

Options are available to the test user that, while not wholly preventative, may reduce the incidence of test-takers falsifying results. Passwords and logins may be administered after identifying personal information is registered, and a statement attached to the registration outlining the disqualifying consequences of falsification.[16] The test designer may also add code into the site that logs the internet protocol (IP) address of the test-taker for identification purposes, or to prevent multiple test access.[17]

Statistical authentication methods, such as re-testing IBT short-listed candidates in a supervised environment and comparing this performance with the original internet score have been proposed.[18] However, statistical comparison of these scores to accurately identify falsification is fraught with error. In examining two statistical authenticity classification methods, it has been concluded that classification accuracy is impacted by the size and precision of item pools, the increment between the test-taker pre and post score, the number of dimensions sampled in the test battery, and the length of the initial test.[19] The potential inaccuracy in these methods of classification introduces significant ethical and legal ramifications if test-taker authenticity were in question. In addition, requiring a supervised post-test lessens the economic and resource advantages that are expected when introducing IBT. As yet, no robust solution has been provided to the issue of test-taker authenticity, if the test is delivered remotely and not proctored.

Challenge 4: It Must be Fair

When administering psychological selection tests, it is best practice to keep test conditions as invariant as possible from one administration to the next, allowing meaningful and equitable interpretation of the test results, and comparison with an established normative standard. Test scores may vary significantly between applicants undertaking testing in a remote uncontrolled environment (e.g., at home) compared to a standardized environment (e.g., secure test centre); thus introducing potentially inequitable comparisons.

The perceived equity of an IBT is also important to the efficacy of the recruitment and selection process. The perception of inequity can lead to negative feelings about the organization including decreased reapplication, decreased recommendations, and lower job attraction.[20] It has been demonstrated that applicants report lower user-friendliness, and reduced perception of fairness for tests undertaken in remote, unsupervised environments.[21] It has been further demonstrated that applicants' information privacy concerns from remotely administered internet selection tests were negatively related to their feelings of procedural justice of the selection process, which in turn affected test-taker motivation, organizational attraction and intent toward the organization.[22] Applicants' negative reactions to the use of internet-based procedures, particularly for high stakes decisions, can have serious consequences, including legal contest to the equity of the selection process and, potentially, a decrease in recruitment pools.

Challenge 5: It Must be Effective

If a valid and reliable test is converted to internet delivery from other modes of administration, such as pencil-and-paper (PP), it cannot be taken for granted that this test will be psychometrically equivalent.[23] There are many factors that may threaten both the reliability and predictive validity of a test when administered over the internet. For example, hardware variations such as differing screen size and internet access speed have a demonstrated effect on performance in verbal and mathematical abilities tests;[24] item non-response has been shown to increase with different surface characteristics of the test display;[25] and applicant characteristics, such as computer anxiety, have been shown to negatively impact cognitive test performance.[26]

However, several research studies using non-cognitive tests have found that IBT versions of personality and experience-based inventories reach equivalent levels of reliability and validity to that demonstrated by their PP counterparts.[27] Joinson found that completing tests on the internet decreases the respondent's public self-awareness, while increasing their private self-awareness, thus making responses less socially desirable and more truthful.[28] While these findings are positive for low stakes inventories, the effect may be diminished for high stakes testing, which would require identification. For example, Oswald, Carr & Schmidt have demonstrated that the presence of a supervisor altered responses on personality tests, which may in turn make these tests less reliable.[29]

Ultimately, test reliability, validity and equivalence with other forms of administration must be conducted on a test-by-test basis, and resolution of the factors affecting test performance and equity must be undertaken prior to using IBT.

THE PROMISE OF IBT

Despite these challenges, careful use of IBT, based on a thorough understanding of the limitations outlined above, holds great promise for organizations, including the military. Low stakes internet-delivered inventories to assist career guidance have high utility, in both the accessibility to potential applicants, and honesty of responses applicants appear to give in anonymous, unsupervised administration modes. Where anonymity is not feasible, efforts should be undertaken to ensure identification does not negatively impact responses or applicant perceptions. For example, the British Army's "Pathfinder" requires contact details to be entered after test administration, though before the applicant's results are displayed. Precautions should also be taken to ensure that inventory results are job relevant, and applicant reactions to the advisory process are monitored. IBT is likely to be most effective as a complement to conventional face-to-face career guidance with an experienced military member.

It is clear that for the time being, and consistent with the best practice recommendations provided by the 2005 ITC guidelines, high stakes selection tests should remain in the Supervised or Managed mode of administration, irrespective of the driving technology. These modes ensure, within reason, that the test items are secure; test-taker authenticity (assuming the presentation of suitable identification) is guaranteed; the test conditions are satisfactorily standardized; and the applicants are more confident in the security of their information and the procedural fairness of the selection process. These administration modes do not rule out test delivery via the internet, however equivalent solutions and advantages may be provided by intranet-based test administration that may be more cost-effective for the test user.

So too, while IBT may show promise for test delivery and be considered for pre-screening applicants, the utility of this for the military, compared to other organizations, may be lessened by the recruiting climate. Pre-screening has utility for jobs with high selection ratios (e.g., selection of 30 candidates from, potentially, thousands of applicants), however is less useful and cost-effective for military organizations that, typically, have lower selection ratios and higher recruitment pressures. If IBT pre-screening were logistically and ethically feasible, it may only have utility for high attraction, specialized military jobs. The benefits of the internet for military organizations lie in recruitment, and potentially in the reduction of information gathering required at recruiting centres. This may include having the applicant provide biodata, education, medical history, and potentially undertake a psychopathology pre-screen prior to face-to-face contact with the organization.

As technology develops, solutions to the challenges involved in providing fair, secure and effective IBT may emerge. Continual research, facilitated by regular information exchange, is essential if TTCP nations are to realize the benefits of this technology.

CHAPTER 8

ENDNOTES

1   Dave Bartram, "Internet Recruitment and Selection: Kissing Frogs to find Princes," *International Journal of Selection and Assessment*, Vol. 8, No. 4 (2000), 261-274.

2   Ibid.

3   Jack A. Naglieri, Fritz Drasgow, Mark Schmit, Len Handler, Aurelio Prifitera, Amy Margolis, and Roberto Velasquez, "Psychological Testing on the Internet: New Problems, Old Issues," *American Psychologist*, Vol. 59, No. 3 (2004), 150-162.

4   International Test Commission (2005). International Guidelines on Computer-based and Internet Delivered Testing, 2005 Version. [Online]. Available: <http://www.intestcom.org>.

5   Ibid.

6   Filip Lievens and Michael M. Harris, "Research on Internet Recruiting and Testing: Current Status and Future Directions," *International Review of Industrial and Organizational Psychology*, Vol. 18 (2003), 131-165.

7   International Test Commission.

8   James R. McBride, Arthur F. Paddock, Lauress L. Wise, William J. Strickland, and Brian K. Waters, *Testing Via the Internet: A Literature Review and Analysis of Issues for Department of Defense Internet Testing of the Armed Services Vocational Aptitude Battery (ASVAB) in High Schools* (Seaside, CA: Defense Manpower Data Center Research Report, 2001).

9   Bartram, "Internet Recruitment and Selection".

10   McBride *et al., Testing Via the Internet.*

11   Azy Barak and Nicole English, "Prospects and Limitations of Psychological Testing on the Internet" *Journal of Technology in Human Services*, Vol. 19, No. 2/3 (2002), 65-89.

12   Aimee Williamson, "Online Assessment: Current Issues and Future Views," Paper presented at the *International Test Users' Conference,* Melbourne, VIC., Australia (2004).

13   Bartram, "Internet Recruitment and Selection".

14   Azy Barak, "Psychological Applications on the Internet: A Discipline on the Threshold of a New Millennium," *Applied and Preventative Psychology*, Vol. 8 (1999), 231-245; Naglieri *et al.*, "Psychological Testing on the Internet."

15   McBride *et al., Testing Via the Internet.*

16   John Mooney, "Pre-employment Testing on the Internet: Put Candidates a Click Away and Hire at Modem Speed," *Public Personnel Management,* Vol. 31, No. 1 (2002), 41-52.

17   William C. Schmidt, "The Server Side of Psychology Web Experiments," in Michael H. Birnbaum, ed., *Psychological Experiments on the Internet* (San Diego: Academic Press, 2000).

18   Mooney, "Pre-employment Testing"; S. Dover, "The Impact of On-Line Assessment on Test Takers, Test Results, Psychometric Factors, and Selection System Effectiveness," Paper presented at the *2nd Eurocontrol Selection Seminar on FEAST* (2003).

19   D.O. Segall, "Measuring Test Compromise in High Stakes Computerized Adaptive Testing: A Bayesian Strategy for Surrogate Test-taker Detection," Paper presented at the annual meeting of the *National Council on Measurement in Education,* Seattle, WA, 2001.

20   Ann Marie Ryan and Robert E. Ployhart, "Applicants' Perceptions for Selection Procedures and Decisions: A Critical Review and Agenda for the Future," *Journal of Management*, Vol. 26, No. 3 (2000), 565-606.

21   S.S. Fallaw and G.S. Stokes, "Reactions to Online Selection Systems: Differences by Location," Paper presented at the *19th Annual Meeting of the Society for Industrial and Organizational Psychology*, Chicago, IL, 2004.

22   Tayla N. Bauer, Donald M. Truxillo, Jennifer S. Tucker, Vaunne Weathers, Marilena Bertolino, Berrin Erdogan, and Michael A. Campion, "Selection in the Information Age: The Impact of Computer Experience and Privacy Concerns on Applicant Reactions," *Journal of Management*, Vol. 32 (2006), 601-621.

23   Lee J. Cronbach, *Essentials of Psychological Testing*, 5th ed. (New York: Harper-Collins, 1990).

24   Brent Bridgeman, Mary Louise Lennon, and Altamese Jackenthal, "Effects of Screen Size, Screen Resolution, and Display Rate on Computer-based Test Performance," *Applied Measurement in Education*, Vol. 16, No. 3 (2003), 191-205.

25   Katja L. Manfreda, Zenel Batagelj, and Vasja Vehovar, "Design of Web Survey Questionnaires: Three Basic Experiments", *Journal of Computer Mediated Communication*, Vol. 7, No. 3 (2002). [Online]. Available: <http://www.ascusc.org/jcmc/vol7/issue3/vehovar.html>.

26   S. Smith, Peter Caputi, Hanna Thomas, Nicole Steele, and Alan Twomey, *Assessing the Equivalence of Conventional versus Computer-based Tests of Cognitive Ability in Recruitment and Selection.* (RR11/2002) (Canberra, Australia: Department of Defence. Psychology Research and Technology Group, 2002).

27   Tom Buchanan and John L. Smith, "Using the Internet for Psychological Research: Personality Testing on the World Wide Web," *British Journal of Psychology,* Vol. 90 (1999), 125-144; Karen A. Pasveer and John H. Ellard, "The Making of a Personality Inventory: Help from the WWW," *Behaviour Research Methods, Instruments and Computers,* Vol. 30 (1998), 309-313; Robert E. Ployhart, Jeff A. Weekly, Brian C. Holtz, and Cary Kemp, "Web-based and Paper-and-pencil Testing of Applicants in a Proctored Setting: Are Personality, Biodata, and Situational Judgement Tests Comparable?" *Personnel Psychology*, Vol. 56, No. 3 (2003), 733-752; D.H. Reynolds, E.F. Sinar, and A.C. McClough, "Evaluation of a Web-based Selection Procedure." In N.J. Mondragon (Chair), "Beyond the Demo: The Empirical Nature of Technology-Based Assessments," Symposium presented at the *15th Annual Conference of the Society for Industrial and Organisational Psychology*, New Orleans, LA, 2000; Jesus F. Salgado and Silvia Moscoso, "Internet-based Personality Testing: Equivalence of Measures and Assesses' Perceptions and Reactions," *International Journal of Selection and Assessment*, Vol. 11, No. 2/3 (2003), 194-205.

28   Adam Joinson, "Social Desirability, Anonymity and Internet-based Questionnaires," *Behaviour Research Methods, Instruments and Computers*, Vol. 31, No. 3 (1999), 433-438.

29   F.L. Oswald, J.Z. Carr and A.M. Schmidt, "The Medium and the Message: Dual Effects of Supervision and Web-based Testing on Measurement Equivalence for Ability and Personality Measures," in F.L. Oswald (Chair), "Computers = good? How Test-user and Test-taker Perceptions Affect Technology-based Employment Testing," Symposium presented at the *16th Annual Conference of the Society for Industrial and Organizational Psychology*, San Diego, CA, 2001.

CHAPTER 9

PERFORMANCE APPRAISAL

TONIA S. HEFFNER and CHAD I. PEDDIE
U.S. Army Research Institute for the Behavioural and Social Sciences

Performance appraisals are used routinely in organizations (military and civilian) for decisions regarding promotion, compensation, employee feedback, training needs assessment, and validation of personnel selection techniques.[1] Performance appraisal is defined as "activities through which organizations seek to assess employees and develop their competence, enhance performance, and distribute rewards"[2] and, more specifically, as "the system whereby an organization assigns some 'score' to indicate the level of performance of a target person or group".[3] Across the many available definitions of performance appraisal, the common tenet is the evaluation of an employee to demonstrate accomplishment of tasks and responsibilities related to the employee's organizational position.

The primary purposes of performance appraisal are two-fold, development and evaluation.[4] The developmental performance appraisal focuses on providing feedback, identifying training needs, determining work assignments, and identifying performance strengths and weaknesses. The purpose of a developmental performance appraisal is to improve the employee's contributions to the organization.[5] In contrast to developmental appraisals that focus on aiding the individual, evaluative appraisals have a comparative perspective.[6] An employee's performance is compared to that of others or to an organizational standard. Evaluative appraisals focus on organizational decisions related to employee compensation, promotion, transition, and termination.[7]

CHAPTER 9

THE PERFORMANCE CONSTRUCT

The objective of performance appraisal is to assess the level of performance displayed by an employee. Broadly, job performance is how well an individual contributes to the organization's success. However, job performance is considered to be relatively complex.[8] Three different ways of looking at job behaviour have been identified: task performance, organizational citizenship behaviour, and counterproductive work behaviour. While these generally represent different kinds of behaviour, there are some behaviours which could fall into one or another of these categories, depending on one's perspective.

TASK PERFORMANCE

The prevailing task performance model, characterizes job performance as the units through which individuals contribute to work.[9] The task performance model details a multidimensional construct that captures the nature of most jobs. This model has eight dimensions: *job-specific task proficiency, non-job-specific task proficiency, written and oral communication, demonstration of effort, maintenance of personal discipline, maintenance of peer and team performance, leadership, and management* (see Table 9.1).[10] Further research resulted in the addition of a ninth dimension, adaptability, to capture the dynamic, changing environment in the modern workplace.[11]

Job-specific Task Proficiency	The degree to which the individual executes the individuating performance elements that compose the core technical requirements of jobs.
Non-job-specific Task Proficiency	The degree to which the individual executes the general, non-job specific performance elements that are used by most jobs in an organization.
Written and Oral Communication	The degree to which an individual can effectively convey concepts and ideas to others.
Demonstration of Effort	The degree to which an individual is engaged with work responsibilities and the persistence and intensity demonstrated toward completion of tasks.

114

Maintenance of Personal Discipline	The degree to which an individual avoids negative activities (e.g. alcohol abuse, tardiness, policy violations).
Maintenance of Peer and Team Performance	The degree to which an individual supports and lends guidance to peers. Additionally this dimension captures the degree to which one assists in the cohesive functioning of work groups and units.
Leadership	The degree to which an individual persuades and influences peers and subordinates during in-person, face-to-face interactions.
Management	The degree to which an individual accounts for administrative functions of value to the work unit that do not involve the direct supervision of others (e.g., setting organizational goals, coordinating labour, monitoring organizational resources and progress, and managing finances).
Adaptability	The efficiency with which organizational members manage new work experiences.

TABLE 9.1: Dimensions of Task Performance

ORGANIZATIONAL CITIZENSHIP BEHAVIOUR

Organizational citizenship behaviour, another aspect of job performance, is defined as "individual behaviour that is discretionary, not directly or explicitly recognized by the formal reward system, and that in the aggregate promotes the effective functioning of the organization".[12] Organizational citizenship behaviours are critical to group and organizational functioning but are not traditionally part of the employee's job description. Organizational citizenship behaviours include helping others, providing mentoring, maintaining common work areas, and performing activities that help bolster esprit de corps. Although the *maintenance of peer and team performance* dimension of the task performance model captures some aspects of organizational citizenship behaviours, this perspective has expanded the scope to include a broader range of behaviours.

COUNTERPRODUCTIVE WORK BEHAVIOUR

Counterproductive work behaviour, a third and relatively distinct aspect of job performance, is behaviour initiated with the intention of harming the organization and/or people within the organization.[13] Counterproductive work behaviours go beyond the lack of organizational citizenship behaviours or maintenance of personal discipline from the task performance model. Whereas an employee who lacks organizational citizenship behaviour or is low on maintenance of personal discipline is likely viewed as indifferent to co-workers and the organization, employees who exhibit counterproductive work behaviours are intentionally wronging peers and the organization. Counterproductive work behaviours, which are grouped into five categories, range in magnitude within each category from minor to severe:[14]

- Abuse (interpersonally directed harmful behaviours);

- Production deviance (behaviour aimed at disrupting work-flow);

- Sabotage (destruction of equipment and resources owned by the organization);

- Theft (deliberately assuming possession of equipment and resources owned by the organization); and

- Withdrawal (avoidance of work and work-related activities).

SUMMARY

The three types of job performance, task performance, organizational citizenship behaviours, and counterproductive work behaviours, describe the behaviours that employees can exhibit. The task performance model focuses on the traditional or typical work behaviours such as those found in a job description along with some acknowledgement of organizational citizenship behaviour and counterproductive work behaviour. The organizational citizenship behaviour and counterproductive work behaviour components expand and enhance the task performance model to include both beneficial and detrimental employee behaviours that impact the attainment of organizational goals. Depending on the employee's organizational role and the organization's values, most or all of the behaviours must be assessed to have an accurate and encompassing performance appraisal.

ASSESSING JOB PERFORMANCE

The key to any performance appraisal is the assessment of job performance. A wealth of research studies has investigated performance using supervisory ratings, productivity indices, absenteeism, turnover, salary, and promotion as representations of performance.[15] The general conclusion from this body of research is that each outcome measure has some utility depending on the job being assessed, the objective of the performance appraisal, and the organization's goals.

THE CRITERION PROBLEM

Although a multitude of performance measures may be available, the critical decision for the organization is to select the measures that provide the most meaningful information about the employee's performance. This leads to what is known as the "criterion problem" – the problem of how to get the right outcome measures. A "criterion" is simply some measure of performance, or outcome measure, and is essential to determine the performance of individuals.[16]

The criterion problem is driven by three major issues. First, a pure measure of job performance is not possible, thus we employ criteria to represent performance. In so doing, the use of these criteria, "require additional translations between concepts and measurement operations".[17] In other words, the criteria that are measured may be the best that can be derived, but likely will only capture some aspects of an employee's true performance. For example, measures of job effort could include amount of time spent on task, number of tasks completed, or supervisor and/or peer ratings, each of which taps some aspect of effort.

A second issue for criteria relates to the "overlap" between what the outcome measures capture and the full range of performance behaviours. There tends to be a good deal of incongruence between the dimensions of the criteria and the entire job performance construct. Often the available outcome measures only tap a few of the many dimensions within the three types of job performance. Many dimensions are not assessed or are poorly assessed despite research and common observation showing that these dimensions are important to the vast majority of jobs. It is not always possible or practical to have criteria for each dimension so the overall performance appraisal will be incomplete. Conversely, for some dimensions there might be multiple criteria that can be used, but these criteria may vary in quality. Referring to the measures of job effort above, research and operational use of supervisor and peer ratings demonstrate that they sometimes are quite divergent. One rater is likely more accurate than the other, but it can be complicated to determine which rating should be used in the performance appraisal.

Finally, a related issue is data availability. A comprehensive data capture on every job performance dimension on a daily, or even weekly or monthly, basis is impractical for most organizations and unnecessary for an accurate performance appraisal. However, to obtain an accurate performance appraisal, measures must be available for all of the critical job performance dimensions.

ADDRESSING THE CRITERION PROBLEM

To address the criterion problem, performance measures must be relevant, reliable, sensitive, and practical.[18] Relevant measures are those that reflect true job performance. It is not informative to assess the number of items produced if the employee works on an assembly line and everyone produces the same number. Likewise, computers make it possible to assess everyone on typing speed, but typing speed is not relevant for most jobs. Therefore, it is important to identify the most critical dimensions of performance, typically through job analysis (see chapter 1), to ensure that the performance appraisal is as comprehensive as necessary. Early development of the performance appraisal system can identify which types of data are most critical to collect in advance of the actual evaluation taking place. For example, if written and oral communication are critical aspects of the employee's job, then some data must be captured on this dimension for an accurate performance appraisal.

The performance measure must be reliable. It is critical that the performance measure is assessing what it is intended to assess. A job knowledge test should assess the critical aspects of the job, not irrelevant information. Individual performance can vary over time and thus averaging over these time periods provides a more accurate, or reliable, assessment of performance. For example, military recruiting is impacted by the academic school year. Counting the number of accessions a recruiter has in May provides a very different picture from his or her accessions in December. Averaging across the year will provide a more accurate measure of job performance. Further, performance measures can be influenced by events outside of the employee's control, such as geographic location for a recruiter, that do not reflect true job performance and must be accounted for in the performance appraisal.

Performance measures also must be able to discriminate between good and poor performers. That is to say, they must be sensitive enough to detect those differences that actually exist. If everyone is required to meet a standard, then a measure based on that standard may not be very informative. For example, if everyone is required to do fifty push-ups then, unless you look at some other measure such as number of attempts or time to reach the standard, it provides little information for performance assessment. Performance measures also need to be sensitive to the strengths and weaknesses of individuals. As described above, job performance is multidimensional and employees vary on these dimensions. Often, however, performance evaluations based on ratings are made on a single rating scale or averaged across rating scales which can mask the true strengths and weakness of, and therefore differences between, employees.

Finally, a performance measure must be practical and available. Monitoring and recording the data cannot place undue burden on the individual or supervisory personnel or it likely will be incomplete and unreliable. One of the greatest challenges can be to identify existing data that can be molded into performance measures. Databases are often incomplete, inaccurate, out of date, or insufficient to provide relevant information. It can require a delicate balancing act to obtain the necessary performance measures without creating undue burden on the supervisor or on the organization.

SUMMARY

One of the greatest challenges of designing and implementing a performance appraisal system is to identify and/or develop the right outcome measures. The outcome measures need to be relevant, reliable, sensitive, and practical yet simultaneously reflect the employee's performance. To use only what is readily available often means overlooking critical performance dimensions, leading to less than accurate performance appraisals.

OBJECTIVE AND SUBJECTIVE MEASURES OF PERFORMANCE

Job performance can be assessed using either "objective" or "subjective" outcome measures. Objective measures use some work product, outcome, or behaviour (e.g. sales volume, patients seen, calls processed) to measure performance. In contrast, subjective measures of performance are composed of ratings of work quality demonstrated by an employee and may come from a number of sources (e.g., supervisors, peers, self, clients). The appropriateness of any measure, whether objective and subjective, depends on its relevance, reliability, sensitivity, and practicality. Each outcome measure has limitations and the best approach is the use of multiple measures to reflect as many of the task dimensions, as well as organizational citizenship behaviours and counterproductive work behaviours, as possible. The broader the scope of measurement, the more complete the picture of an individual's performance will be.

OBJECTIVE MEASURES

Examples of objective performance measures include output, quality, lost time, and trainability/promotability (see Table 9.2). Data used in these metrics do vary over time[19] and best practices suggest the averaging of data over multiple time points. Output measures consist of the tallies of units processed (e.g. items sold, dollars generated, goods produced). Output measures often are tracked and recorded in organizations and frequently are used in performance appraisals. They most closely reflect *job-specific task proficiency, non-job-specific task proficiency*, and *demonstration of effort* from the task performance model.

Quality measures reflect unacceptable work that detracts from organizational goals. Depending on the job, some quality measures readily can be obtained from organizational records. For example, the number of complaints a customer service representative receives can be recorded. For other jobs, however, this can be more challenging such as tallying the time cost of editing a poorly written report. Quality measures can reflect most of the task performance dimensions as well as organizational citizenship and counterproductive work behaviours depending on the focus of the measure, the employee's skills, and the employee's motivation.

121

Lost time measures assess the lack of contribution of an employee. Many lost time measures are available from organizational records and are frequently used in performance appraisals. From the task performance model, lost time measures can indicate *demonstration of effort, maintenance of peer and team performance*, and *adaptability*, as well as organizational citizenship and counterproductive work behaviours.

OBJECTIVE PERFORMANCE MEASURES	
Output measures	# of items produced # of items sold Amount of revenue generated # of items processed
Quality measures	# of errors # of complaints Amount of scrap, rework, or breakage Cost of unacceptable work
Lost time	# of absences # of tardies # of unauthorized/lengthy breaks Amount of turnover # of accidents
Trainability/promotability	Time to reach performance standard Level of proficiency Rate of salary increase # of promotions in a set time Time between promotions
SUBJECTIVE PERFORMANCE MEASURES	
Performance rating	Self ratings Peer ratings Subordinate ratings Supervisor ratings Client/customer ratings

Adapted from W.F. Cascio, *Applied Psychology in Human Resource Management*, (Upper Saddle River, NJ: Prentice Hall, 1998). Copyright 1998 by Prentice-Hall, Inc.

TABLE 9.2: Common Performance Measures

Many trainability/promotability are available from organizational records. Within trainability/promotability, however, objective job knowledge assessments and work samples can be the most informative, but are the most resource-intensive. Job knowledge assessments, as implied by the name, measure the degree of declarative knowledge (how much is known) and procedural knowledge (how to do the task) employees have about a particular job. Work samples are akin to higher fidelity simulations in which employee performance is assessed on presented tasks (representing actual role responsibilities). Trainability/promotability measures focus on *job-specific task proficiency* and *non-job specific task proficiency*, in particular, but can represent all of the performance dimensions because promotions usually are based on an employee's overall performance.

SUBJECTIVE MEASURES

Frequent sources of subjective performance measurement include ratings or evaluations provided by supervisors, peers, subordinates, clients/customers, and the employee. Sometimes ratings are collected from several sources to conduct a 360 degree evaluation. Ratings are particularly useful for jobs where objective measures are limited, such as supervisory positions. They are commonly accepted, and even expected, by most employees. Performance ratings also serve to engage employees, supervisors, and subordinates in the performance appraisal process by providing them a "voice" into the evaluation where they can highlight strengths and explain weaknesses.

Subjective measures rely on observation and judgment, both of which can be intentionally or unintentionally biased. Rater errors include leniency/severity, central tendency, and halo.[20] Leniency/severity occurs when the raters consistently give high or low ratings regardless of the actual performance of the employee. Leniency or severity can occur across all of the rating dimensions for a single employee or across all employees. Although it may initially seem that leniency or severity is intentional, it is sometimes unintentional. The rater is not intentionally trying to aid or harm his or her employees in relation to other employees in the organization. It is just that he or she has a different conceptualization of what the rating dimension means or a different standard for evaluating performance. For example, one rater of written communication may consider getting the critical points across as high performance whereas another rater may require correct grammar and punctuation necessary for high performance.

Central tendency is the inclination to provide average ratings, either for all dimensions for a particular employee or for all employees, regardless of the particular strengths and weakness of those employees. Central tendency can happen for a variety of reasons including a) the rater may not have observed the employee's performance, b) the rater does not like to make distinctions between employee performance, or c) the rater has concerns about the uses of the performance appraisals.

Halo arises when raters focus on the particularly good or poor dimensions and allow the assessment of these features to represent the ratee as a whole. For example, if an employee is technically very proficient but has a difficult time working well with peers, a rater may be swayed by technical proficiency to rate the employee high on all performance dimensions. Halo also can occur if the rater is influenced to give higher or lower ratings by a particularly salient event such as an average employee performing particularly well just before the performance appraisal is conducted.

Rater errors and bias combine to distort the accuracy of performance appraisals. Two common methods to reduce errors and bias are to use structured rating scales and to provide rater training.

Structured Rating Scales. The most frequently used structured ratings scales are some variation of behaviourally anchored rating scales

(BARS). BARS are used to provide a common metric for raters to use to evaluate an employee's performance. BARS typically have three characteristics (see Figure 9.1). The title and/or question provide a general description of the rating dimension. The rating dimensions usually are identified and developed through interviews with subject matter experts as part of the job analysis process. Examples of behaviour, known as "anchors", at low, moderate, and high performance levels provide a common standard for evaluating employees and help reduce potential bias. These, too, are usually gathered from subject matter experts. The final characteristic is the numerical rating scale. Rating scales typically range from 1-3 to 1-9 points. The structure provided by BARS seeks to reduce a portion of the subjectivity that is inherent to judgemental measurement.[21] By presenting a common metric, it provides a standard for all raters and makes it easier to compare employees.

Rater Training. Another method to reduce bias is to provide rater training. Rater training programs typically provide trainees with definitions and examples of the more commonly committed rater errors and present suggestions for ways to avoid these errors. A specific type of rater training, frame-of-reference (FOR) training, has demonstrated the most accuracy.[22] FOR training can be provided interactively or through media (videos, slides, web-based). FOR training provides raters with detailed information on the distinctions between all performance dimensions to be evaluated. The dimensions are not only described, but the distinctions between potentially overlapping dimensions are clearly delimited. Like the written descriptions in BARS, rater trainees are presented with examples of specific behaviours along with descriptions of effectiveness (low, moderate, high performance) to guide accurate judgement of observed behaviours. In sum, the primary objective of FOR training is the development of raters who evaluate performance using shared conceptualizations of performance without the errors of untrained raters.

Learns to Provide Emergency Care						
How well has the soldier learned to provide emergency care?						
1	2	3	4	5	6	7
• Freezes or gets confused in stressful/emergency situations; cannot follow directions from others.		• Usually stays calm in stressful/emergency situations; may need direction from others.			• Takes control in stressful/emergency situations; knows what to do and gets started on tasks.	
• Fails to correctly determine treatment priority; treats less severely injured patients first.		• Correctly determines severity of injury or illness and usually requests assistance when necessary.			• Quickly and accurately determines treatment priority; always requests assistance when necessary.	
• Provides improper treatment to patients, which may endanger their survival or safety.		• Provides sufficient treatment to ensure patients' comfort and safety.			• Efficiently provides treatment to patients which ensures their safety and improves their chances for survival.	
• Uses pressure dressings or tourniquets improperly, or fails to use them when needed; lacks knowledge of special life saving techniques and equipment.		• Correctly uses pressure dressings or tourniquets; uses special life saving techniques and equipment in emergency situations.			• Quickly and correctly uses pressure dressings and tourniquets; expertly uses special life saving techniques and equipment in emergency situations.	

FIGURE 9.1: BARS Scale for an Entry-level Medic

CONSIDERATIONS FOR PERFORMANCE APPRAISAL

Although critical to personnel management systems, the performance appraisal processes have to take into account multiple considerations. Some of these have already been described, including selecting the best measures, gathering the best data, and planning in advance.

As briefly mentioned earlier, the reactions of ratees to the performance appraisal process, regardless of the performance appraisal "score," can have impacts that are far reaching (e.g., personnel attitudes, feedback acceptance, supervisor attitudes, subsequent performance, the appraisal itself).[23] There is a strong relationship between the amount of participation and "voice" the employee has in the performance appraisal process and how positively the employee reacts to the process.[24] Not surprisingly, developmental appraisals are generally viewed more positively by employees than evaluative appraisals.[25]

The performance appraisal process and outcomes predict employee attitudes not only towards the process itself, but also toward supervisors and the job.[26] Performance appraisal systems that are perceived as fair by employees have been associated with increased workforce commitment to, and individual goal alignment with, the organization.[27] In addition, positively viewed performance appraisal systems are related to the facilitation of social exchange and reciprocity between ratees and supervisors.[28] In other words, those rated generally seem to value the organization's mission and are less guarded in interactions with others when the performance appraisal process is seen as fair.

Another consideration is that the changing nature of work and work environments impacts the complexity of performance measurement. Many tasks once assigned to individuals are now accomplished as a team. This team structure presents novel challenges to performance assessment in that performance must represent the interdependent contributions of individuals. The performance appraisal process must use assessment procedures that balance effective team performance information with individual contributions. Perceptions of fairness may arise when the appraisals of higher performers are subjected to decrements due to the performance levels of less effective team members.

CONCLUSION

The performance appraisal process is an important element of personnel management but obtaining accurate, complete performance appraisals is a complex task. Job performance is multi-dimensional, consisting of task performance, organizational citizenship behaviour, and counterproductive work behaviour. Gathering the best and most comprehensive data is critical but challenging. It requires advance planning, thorough job analysis, and commitment from organizational members. The pay-off, however, is great. Not only can the organizational managers identify who are the high performing members and who would benefit from developmental activities, but they also can increase employee performance and attitudes through a strong and open performance appraisal process.

ENDNOTES

1   Ted H. Shore, Janet S. Adams, and Armen Tashchian, "Effects of Self-appraisal Information, Appraisal Purpose, and Feedback Target on Performance Appraisal Ratings," *Journal of Business and Psychology*, Vol. 12 (1998), 283-298; Kevin J. Williams, Angelo S. DeNisi, Allyn G. Blencoe, and Thomas P. Cafferty, "The Role of Appraisal Purpose: Effects of Purpose on Information Acquisition and Utilization," *Organizational Behavior and Human Decision Processes*, Vol. 35 (1985), 314-329; Sheldon Zedeck and Wayne F. Cascio, "Performance Appraisal Decisions as a Function of Rater Training and Purpose of the Appraisal," *Journal of Applied Psychology*, Vol. 67 (1982), 752-758.

2   Clive Fletcher, "Performance Appraisal and Management: The Developing Research Agenda," *Journal of Occupational and Organizational Psychology*, Vol. 73 (2001), 473.

3   Angelo S. DeNisi, "Performance Appraisal and Performance Management: A Multilevel Analysis," in Katherine J. Klein and Steve Kozlowski, eds., *Multilevel Theory, Research and Methods in Organizations*, (San Francisco: Jossey-Bass, 2000), 121.

4   Jeanette N. Cleveland, Kevin R. Murphy, and Richard E. Williams, "Multiple Uses of Performance Appraisal: Prevalence and Correlates," *Journal of Applied Psychology*, Vol. 74 (1989), 130-135; Bard Kuvaas, "Different Relationships Between Perceptions of Developmental Performance Appraisal and Work Performance," *Personnel Review*, Vol. 36 (2007), 378-397.

5   Jeffrey B. Arthur, "Effects of Human Resource Systems on Manufacturing Performance and Turnover," *Academy of Management Journal*, Vol. 37 (1994), 670-687; Christopher J. Collins and Ken G. Smith, "Knowledge Exchange and Combination: "The Role of Human Resource Practices in the Performance of High-technology Firms," *Academy of Management Journal*, Vol. 49 (2006), 544-560; Riki Takeuchi, David P. Lepak, Heli Wang, and Kazuo Takeuchi, "An Empirical Examination of the Mechanisms Mediating Between High-performance Work Systems and the Performance of Japanese Organizations," *Journal of Applied Psychology*, Vol. 92 (2007), 1069-1083.

6   Tingting Chen, Peiguan Wu, and Kwok Leung, "Individual Performance Appraisal and Appraisee Reactions to Workgroups: The Mediating Role of Goal Interdependence and the Moderating Role of Procedural Justice," *Personnel Review*, Vol. 40 (2011), 87-105.

7   Wendy R. Boswell and John W. Boudreau, "Employee Satisfaction with Performance Appraisals and Appraisers: The Role of Perceived Appraisal Use," *Human Resource Development Quarterly*, Vol. 11 (2000), 283-299.

8   J.P. Campbell, R.A. McCloy, S.H. Oppler, and C.E. Sager, "A Theory of Performance," in N. Schmitt and Walter C. Borman, eds., *Personnel Selection in Organizations* (San Francisco, CA: Jossey-Bass, 1993), 35-70; Dennis W. Organ, *Organizational Citizenship Behavior* (Lexington, MA: D.C. Health, 1988); Paul E. Spector and S. Fox "A Model of Counterproductive Work Behaviour," in S. Fox and Paul E. Spector, eds., *Counterproductive Workplace Behavior: Investigations of Actors and Targets* (Washington, DC: APA, 2005), 151-174.

9   Campbell *et al.*, "A Theory of Performance".

10   Ibid.

11   D.R. Ilgen and E.D. Pulakos, "Employee Performance in Today's Organizations," in D.R. Ilgen and E.D, Pulakos, eds., *The Changing Nature of Work Performance: Implications for Staffing, Motivation, and Development* (San Francisco: Jossey-Bass, 1999), 1-20; Elaine D. Pulakos, Sharon Arad, Michelle A. Donovan, and Kevin E. Plamondon, "Adaptability in the Workplace: Development of a Taxonomy of Adaptive Performance," *Journal of Applied Psychology*, Vol. 85 (2000), 612-624.

12   Organ, *Organizational Citizenship Behaviour*, 4.

13   Spector and Fox, "A Model of Counterproductive Work Behaviour".

14   Paul E. Spector, Suzy Fox, Lisa M. Penney, Kari Bruursema, Angeline Goh, and Stacey Kessler, "The Dimensionality of Counterproductivity: Are All Counterproductive Behaviors Created Equal?" *Journal of Vocational Behavior*, Vol. 68 (2006), 446-460.

15   S.J. Motowidlo, W.C. Borman, D.R. Ilgen and R.J. Klimoski, eds, *Handbook of Psychology: Industrial and Organizational Psychology*, Vol. 12 (Hoboken, NJ: John Wiley & Sons Inc., 2003).

16   N.W. Schmitt and R.J. Klimoski, *Research Methods in Human Resources Management* (Cincinnati, OH: South-Western, 1991).

17   James T. Austin and Peter Villanova, "The Criterion Problem: 1917-1992," *Journal of Applied Psychology*, Vol. 77 (1992), 863.

18   Wayne F. Cascio, *Applied Psychology in Human Resource Management*. (Upper Saddle River, NJ: Prentice Hall, 1998).

19   Harold F. Rothe, "Output Rates Among Industrial Employees," *Journal of Applied Psychology*, Vol. 63 (1978), 40-46.

20   R.M. Guion, *Assessment, Measurement, and Prediction for Personnel Decisions*, 2nd ed. (New York: Routledge, 2011).

21   Landy and Farr, 1980; Patricia Cain Smith and L. M. Kendall, "Retranslation of Expectations: An Approach to the Construction of Unambiguous Anchors for Rating Scales" *Journal of Applied Psychology*, Vol. 47 (1963), 149-155.

22   Elaine D. Pulakos, "A Comparison of Rater Training Programs: Error Training and Accuracy Training," *Journal of Applied Psychology* 69 (1984), 581-558; David J. Woehr and Allen I. Huffcutt, "Rater Training for Performance Appraisal: A Quantitative Review," *Journal of Occupational and Organizational Psychology*, Vol. 67 (1994), 189-205.

23   Michelle Brown and John Benson, "Rated to Exhaustion? Reactions to Performance Appraisal Processes," *Industrial Relations Journal,* Vol. 34 (2003), 76-81; Douglas H. Flint, "The Role of Organisational Justice in Multi-source Performance Appraisal: Theory-based Application and Direction for Research," *Human Resource Management Review*, Vol. 9 (1999), 1-20; Kwok Leung, Steven Su, and Michael W. Morris, "When is Criticism not Constructive? The Roles of Fairness Perceptions and Dispositional Attributions in Employee Acceptance of Critical Supervisory Feedback," *Human Relations,* Vol. 54 (2001), 1155-1187; Paul E. Levy and Jane R. Williams, "The Social Context of Performance Appraisal," *Journal of Management* (Annual Review Issue), Vol. 30 (2004), 881-905.

24   Brian D. Cawley, Lisa M. Keeping, and Paul E. Levy, "Participation in the Performance Appraisal Process and Employee Reactions: A Meta-analytic Review of Field Investigations," *Journal of Applied Psychology*, Vol. 83 (1998), 615-633.

25   Boswell and Boudreau, "Employee Satisfaction with Performance Appraisals".

26.   James L. Jordan and Deovina B. Nasis, "Preferences for Performance-appraisal Based on Method Used, Type of Rater, and Purpose of Evaluation," *Psychological Reports*, Vol. 70 (1992), 963-969; Herbert H. Meyer, Emanuel Kay, and John R. P. French Jr., "Split Roles in Performance Appraisal," *Harvard Business Review,* Vol. 43 (1965), 123-129; J. Bruce Prince and Edward E. Lawler, "Does Salary Discussion Hurt the Developmental Performance Appraisal?" *Organizational Behavior and Human Resource Decision Processes*, Vol. 37 (1986), 357-375.

27   Arthur, "Effects of Human Resource Systems".

28   Collins and Smith, "Knowledge Exchange and Combination"; Takeuchi *et al.*, "An Empirical Examination".

CHAPTER 10

THE MILITARY FAMILY: CONTEMPORARY CHALLENGES

SANELA DURSUN and **KERRY SUDOM**
Director General Military Personnel Research and Analysis
Department of National Defence, Canada

INTRODUCTION

It is a well-known fact that work and family life can interact with one another, such that individuals who enjoy a healthy, happy family life are more likely to be committed, focused and effective at work. Conversely, conflict between work and family life can have a negative impact on well-being, and has been linked to alcohol use, poor health, low job satisfaction, burnout, increased turnover, and decreased performance.[1]

Perhaps more than other type of organizations, the military can have a pervasive influence on family life. Unlike most organizations, the member's family is generally highly involved in the culture and organization of the military.[2] Military life places a number of unique and extremely intense demands on its members and their families, including frequent separations, relocations, risks of injury or death, long hours, changeable work schedules, and isolation from civilian society.[3] Military institutions challenge families in ways that would be unimaginable in most civilian occupations. These realities, combined with isolation from traditional sources of support, such as extended families, close friends, and stable community relationships,[4] can lead to significant amounts of stress for military families. This chapter will discuss the unique challenges faced by military families and highlight the importance of families for military members and for the military organization as a whole. As well, several trends in the military and in society in general, which have led to increased recognition of the importance of families in the military, will be discussed.

CHALLENGES EXPERIENCED BY MILITARY FAMILIES: DEPLOYMENT AND DUTY-RELATED SEPARATION

Military spouses face a number of unique stressors as they attempt to meet the demands placed upon them by the military institution. Aspects of military life which can influence the well-being of family members include frequent relocations, temporary housing, spousal unemployment and underemployment, separations, deployments to hostile situations, and long and often unpredictable work hours. Any combination of these factors may be a source of stress for military families. Perhaps the most significant among these stressors is the separation of family members due to operational deployments.[5]

Military deployments and duty-related separations are defining experiences for military members and their families. Separations often entail a reorganization of family roles and routines as the spouse remaining at home adjusts to the partner's absence. Stressors may include strain on the marital relationship, childcare concerns, changes in children's wellbeing, difficulties accessing military services, and practical issues such as those surrounding home and car maintenance.[6] Non-deployed spouses may experience loneliness, anger and depression as well as headaches, weight change and sleep disturbances.[7] Coupled with a recent relocation, imminent childbirth, or spouse unemployment, the partners of military members may have a difficult time adjusting to separations.

Deployment and duty-related separations are challenging for families, and stress is a normal response during such separations.[8] Families go through a distinct stage process when a member is deployed: reflecting the pre-deployment, deployment, and post-deployment phases.[9] Not surprisingly, what is perceived as stressful before a deployment differs from what is perceived as stressful during or after a deployment. Spouses of military members go through a number of feelings and experiences throughout this cycle, including initial shock, departure, emotional disintegration, recovery and stabilization, anticipation of the homecoming, reunion and reintegration.[10] Although the views on which deployment phase is the most difficult differ among researchers, it is clear that deployment places both the military member and the spouse remaining at home under considerable stress.

The pre-deployment phase is the stage before military members are deployed to the environment where the operation, mission or exercise is taking place.[11] Researchers have indicated that conflicts in the family are at their peak prior to deployment.[12] Anxiety, apprehension, sadness, and emotional withdrawal are commonly experienced during this time.[13] During the deployment phase, many spouses experience a period of emotional instability and disorganization characterized by feelings of sadness, depression, disorientation, anxiety, loneliness, being overwhelmed, numbness, anger, and relief.[14] There are also physical reactions such as sleep disturbances and other physical health complaints.[15] Children may have a particularly difficult time dealing with a parent's deployment. Research has shown that children have higher levels of depression during deployment,[16] as well as sadness and greater need for discipline.[17]

As the deployment ends, the reintegration phase begins. Post-deployment reunion can be a time of considerable strain for families. In anticipation of homecoming, both excitement and apprehension increase.[18] During the deployment, roles have been redefined, new family systems have developed, and both serving members and their spouses have inevitably changed.[19] The post-deployment phase is typically marked by ambivalence and anxiety,[20] as well as disappointment when the fantasy of the reunion does not materialize.[21] Common experiences in marriages during this time include poor communication, emotional distancing, sexual difficulties and anger.[22] As well, problems such as marital conflict and estrangement, behavioural changes in children, and physical stress symptoms may be evident.[23] Military members who were involved in combat or experienced other traumatic events may introduce the after-effects of these experiences into their family system.[24] The reintegration phase can take up to six months, as the couple and family stabilize their relationships.[25]

IMPORTANCE OF FAMILY SUPPORT FOR MILITARY MEMBERS AND THE MILITARY ORGANIZATION

It is evident from the research above that military life, particularly deployments, can have a negative impact on families. However, it is important that the family is supportive of the military member, and that the relationships within the family remain strong even in the face of such stressors. Supportive relationships, especially from family members, are important for the well-being of military personnel. Research with civilian samples has revealed that marital stress and lack of support from one's spouse were linked to depression.[26] In fact, individuals experiencing marital distress are ten times more likely than happily married people to experience symptoms of depression.[27] Military research has demonstrated similar findings. A survey of Canadian Forcers members revealed that perceived support from one's spouse, and confidence in the spousal relationship, were linked to higher well-being.[28] Furthermore, research conducted with United States soldiers during Operation DESERT STORM found that soldiers who reported higher rates of family problems at home had more psychological symptoms and were less resistant to combat stress syndrome.[29]

In addition to being important for the well-being of military members, spousal support is important for the military organization. CF members who felt that their spouse was supportive of their career reported higher morale and commitment to the military.[30] A variety of research has found that family and marital relationships are related to important organizational outcomes, such as retention, personal morale and readiness.

Several studies in the U.S. military examined the impact of family factors on military members' retention. Spousal support for the service member's reenlistment has an important impact on whether the member will actually remain in the service.[31] In fact, separation from one's family for military reasons was one of the biggest factors affecting decisions to leave the military.[32] Other family variables that affect whether an individual plans to remain in the military include the spouse's attitudes about military life,[33] member and spouse satisfaction with the quality of military life,[34] and member and spouse perception of the extent to which supervisors, co-workers, and the military organization are supportive of families.[35] Research in the CF has pointed out that family considerations, such as availability and quality of family support, and ability to balance work and family life, were some of the greatest factors affecting retention, in that members identified family issues as the number one reason for leaving the military.[36]

Individual readiness, a concept which includes the preparedness of a member's family to deal with the rigors of deployment, has become an even more pressing issue for many Western militaries in recent years with the higher operational tempo that they are experiencing. Many members of the military community believe that family issues can influence readiness. Any military commander can cite examples from his or her own experience of ways in which soldiers' families have fostered or hindered individual and unit readiness. In addition, there is some empirical evidence that family life, specifically, spouses' attitudes toward the military, is associated with members' morale.[37]

The organizational outcomes mentioned above (i.e., organizational commitment, personal morale, operational readiness and turnover intent) are the key components of organizational effectiveness in the military.[38] There is some empirical evidence that family factors may have an impact on all these organizational outcomes.

THE CHANGING FACE OF THE MILITARY

It is clear from the studies cited that families have a significant impact upon the military. It is important, therefore, to understand the interactions between military and family life. Consideration of the impacts of military life on families is important, particularly at a point when several trends, both in the military and in society in general, have functioned to increase attention to the impacts of military life on families. Prior to the 1980s, family issues were not of paramount concern to the military because many members were single. In the late 1980s, Segal characterized the military as a "greedy" institution because of its tremendous demands for the loyalty and commitment of service members and their families.[39] Family members were expected to adapt to these demands and place their unconditional support behind the service member in his/her efforts to successfully accomplish the military mission.

In the past several decades, however, various trends have combined to increase attention on military families. First, the conditions of military family life, to which families are required to adapt, have changed. The total number of members in the CF has steadily decreased over the last 15 years, while the military has become increasingly involved in a variety of multinational peacekeeping and humanitarian assistance missions as well as the most recent combat role in Afghanistan. The recent role of the CF in Afghanistan, and the increased danger associated with it, has created additional stress for both members and their families, since it has resulted in increased time away as well as risk of injury and death.

In addition to the changing nature of CF missions and the resultant increase in family separation, the demographic patterns of military personnel have changed dramatically in recent years. Most notable is the increasing proportion of married military personnel. During the 1980s, following the promulgation of the *Canadian Human Rights Act* and the *Charter of Right and Freedoms*, the CF removed its restrictive age eligibility requirements for entry, thus permitting older Canadians to apply for military service. Recent focus groups conducted with CF service providers identified an emerging trend of increasing numbers of older, already married (or in a common-law relationship) individuals joining the military.[40] Thus, whereas in the past, the majority of personnel entering the military were single, most members are now married.[41] The obvious implication of this trend is that married military members have additional family responsibilities in comparison to their unmarried counterparts. The ability of military members to divide their time and energy between two demanding entities places additional stress on the military member and can have adverse affects on the family. As for the CF as an organization, an increased proportion of married military personnel implies a greater need for policies, programs, and practices to be responsive to family needs, as well as a larger number of individuals who are served by such family programs.

The third notable trend is the fact that in recent decades, women have been fully integrated into all CF roles, including combat. In 1989, a Canadian Human Rights Commission (CHRC) Tribunal directed that all trials of women in non-traditional roles were to cease and that women were to be fully integrated into all CF roles, with the exclusion of service on submarines. In 2001, that last restriction was removed. The proportion of women in the CF has increased substantially since this time. The unique social pressures on women with regards to family, and the increased role that women are playing in the military, make work-family conflict for women in the military a much greater concern. Women now face many of the same conflicts their male counterparts faced when dividing their focus between their family and military career. However, family roles have traditionally been more central for women than for men, and sacrifices made by women were more likely to be expected and considered legitimate. Additionally, because of deeply ingrained career expectations, men may still be reluctant to take on the primary role in the family that is often expected when the mother is a military member.[42] This social dilemma may increase conflict within the family as well as between family and work.

In addition to the above trends related specifically to the military, a number of societal and economic changes have had a significant effect on the military and the relation between military and family life. Of particular interest are changes over the past few decades with regard to gender roles. Although women in general still have a disproportionate responsibility for raising children, men increasingly share this role.[43] The switch from traditional complementary roles, wherein men assumed bread-winning responsibilities and women were primary caretakers for children, to a role-symmetrical model in which men and women can be equally involved in earning and caring, has accentuated the importance of fathers within the lives of their children, not only in terms of the provision of resources, but also with respect to their presence and day-to-day involvement.[44] These changing norms clearly have implications for the tensions between military work and members' domestic responsibilities.[45] Furthermore, such changes of social norms include an increase in dual earner/dual career families. Often, the spouses of the military members are left to manage day-to-day family activities in addition to their work outside the home. However, frequent relocations and separations due to deployment compromise the capacity of military spouses to develop and maintain their own careers, further contributing to family tensions associated with military life.

The changes in military missions, family patterns, gender roles, and general societal and economic trends have led to an increased focus on the families of military members. Recognizing the importance of the family, the CF has adopted the adage, "we recruit a member, but retain a family". As the military family has become more diverse over the last few decades, finding ways to support and strengthen military families is becoming more complex.

CONCLUSION

To the extent that spouses provide a vital resource in the promotion of service members' well-being, readiness, performance and ability to carry out missions, it is crucial to understand how families can maintain and even enhance resiliency during and after military deployments and separations. It has been found that spouses' willingness to support a military career is associated with their own well-being.[46] Therefore, it is important to understand what factors contribute to the well-being of the military spouses and their quality of life. As we have seen, families may undergo significant amounts of stress resulting from military service, especially in relation to separation. Particular characteristics of military spouses, such as independence and use of active coping strategies, can help to reduce the negative consequences of stressors.[47] Furthermore, the negative effects of military family stressors can be reduced by leader support and organizational policies. Research has demonstrated the effectiveness of implementing organizational family-friendly policies and programs.[48] For example, military spouses who perceive that the military recognizes and respects the contribution made by them were less likely to appraise the deployment experience as threatening or stressful, and were more likely to perceive that they were in control and able to cope with the deployment. This, in turn, was associated with greater psychological well-being and satisfaction with life.[49]

Given the extensive amount of time and money required to recruit and train military personnel, it is of the utmost importance that military decision-makers understand the factors that influence the operational effectiveness and career commitments of its members. Only then can they develop and endorse programs and policies that help reduce turnover, increase organizational effectiveness and mission success. It appears as though the well-being of military spouses and the effectiveness of military members are co-dependent constructs, which are directly affected by military service. Therefore, this appears to be a field of research worthy of additional and on-going study.

ENDNOTES

1   Gary A. Adams, Lynda A. King, and Daniel W. King, "Relationships of Job and Family Involvement, Family Social Support, and Work-family Conflict with Job and Life Satisfaction," *Journal of Applied Psychology*, Vol. 81 (1996), 411-420; Michael R. Frone, "Work-family Conflict and Employee Psychiatric Disorders: The National Co-morbidity Survey," *Journal of Applied Psychology*, Vol. 85 (2000), 888-895; Michael R. Frone, Marcia Russell, and Grace M. Barnes, "Work-family Conflict, Gender, and Health-related Outcomes: A Study of Employed Parents in Two Community Samples," *Journal of Occupational Health Psychology*, Vol. 1 (1996), 57-69.

2   Michelle M. Wisecarver, Meredith L. Cracraft and Tonia S. Heffner, *Deployment Consequences: A Review of the Literature and Integration of Findings into a Model of Retention*. ARI Research Report 1845. (Arlington, VA: U.S. Army Research Institute, 2006).

3   M.W. Segal and J.J. Harris, *What We Know About Army Families* (Alexandria, VA: U.S. Army Research Institute for the Behavioral and Social Sciences, 1993).

4   William G. Black, "Military Induced Family Separation: A Stress Reduction Intervention," *Social Work*, Vol. 38, No. 3 (1993), 273-280.

5   D.J. Westhius, "Working with Military Families During Deployments." In James G. Daley, ed., *Social Work Practice in the Military* (New York: Hawthorne, 1999), 217-233.

6   E.W. Van Vranken, L.K. Jellen, K.H.M Knudson, D.H. Marlowe and M.W. Segal, *The Impact of Deployment Separation on Army Families* (Washington, DC: Department of Military Psychiatry, Walter Reed Army Institute of Research, 1984).

7   Ibid.

8   James A. Martin, Mark A. Vaitkus, Malcolm D. Johnson, Louis M. Mikolajek, and Donna L. Ray, "Deployment from Europe: The Family Perspective," in R.J. Ursano

and A.E. Norwood (Eds.), *Emotional Aftermath of the Persian Gulf War: Veterans, Families, Communities, and Nations* (Washington, DC: American Psychiatric Press, 1996), 227-250.

9   Pincus, House, Christensen and Adler, 2001.

10   E. de Soir, *Peace-support Operations and Family Problems: Support Activities to Prevent Culture Shock and Psychosocial Family Trauma*, Paper presented at the NATO / Partnership for Peace Workshop Psychological Readiness for Multinational Operations: Directions for the 21st Century. Heidelberg, Germany (1997).

11   Leora N. Rosen, Kathleen Wright, David Marlowe, Paul Bartone, and Robert K. Gifford, "Gender Differences in Subjective Distress Attributable to Anticipation of Combat Among U.S. Soldiers Deployed to the Persian Gulf during Operation Desert Storm," *Military Medicine*, Vol. 164 (1999), 753-757.

12   Amy B. Adler, Mark A. Vaitkus, and James A. Martin, "Combat Exposure and Posttraumatic Stress Symptomatology Among U.S. Soldiers Deployed to Iraq," *Military Psychology*, Vol. 8 (1996), 1-14.

13   Adrian DuPlessis Van Breda, *Resilience Theory: A Literature Review.* (South African Military Health Service, Military Psychological Institute, Social Work Research & Development, 2001).

14   Pincus *et al.*

15   Kathleen M. Wright, Lolita M. Burrell, Erica D. Schroeder, and Jeffrey L. Thomas, "Military Spouses: Coping with the Fear and the Reality of Service Member Injury and Death," in C.A. Castro, A.B. Adler and C.A. Britt, eds., *Military Life: The Psychology of Serving in Peace and Combat* (Bridgeport, CT: Praeger Security International, 2006), 39-63.

16   Peter S. Jensen, David Martin, and Henry K. Watanabe, "Children's Response to Parental Separation during Operation Desert Storm," *Journal of American Academy of Child and Adolescent Psychiatry*, Vol. 35 (1996), 433-441.

17   L.N. Rosen, J.M. Teitelbaum and D.J. Westhuis, "Children's Reactions to the Desert Storm Deployment: Initial Findings from a Survey of Army Families," *Military Medicine*, Vol. 158 (1993), 465-469.

18   Pincus *et al.*

19   Mady Wechsler Segal, "Military Family Research," in A. D. Mangelsdorff (Ed.), *Psychology in the Service of National Security.* (Washington, DC: American Psychological Association, 2006).

20   Charles R. Figley, "Coping with Stressors on the Home Front," *Journal of Social Issues,* Vol. 49 (1993), 51-71.

21   P. Potts, "Home Sweet Home?" *Air Force Times* (1988), 61-67.

22   B. Wayne Blount, Amos Curry, and Gerald I. Lubin, "Family Separations in the Military," *Military Medicine*, Vol. 157 (1992) 76-80.

23   Jensen *et al.*, "Children's Response to Parental Separation".

24   Figley, "Coping with Stressors".

25   Pincus *et al.*

26   Sheri L. Johnson and Theodore Jacob, "Marital Interactions of Depressed Men and Women," *Journal of Consulting and Clinical Psychology*, Vol. 65 (1997), 15-23.

27   K. Daniel O'Leary, Jennifer L. Christian, and Nancy R. Mendell, "A Closer Look at the Link Between Marital Discord and Depressive Symptomatology," *Journal of Social and Clinical Psychology*, Vol. 13 (1994), 33-41.

28   Sanela Dursun, "Results of the 2005 Spouse Perstempo Survey," Presentation to the Military Family National Advisory Board (2006).

29   J.M. Teitelbaum, "ODS and Post-ODS Divorce and Child Behavior Problems" Paper Presented at the Office of the Secretary of Defense Family Research in-Progress Review, The Pentagon, Washington, DC. (1992).

30   Dursun, "Results of the 2005 Spouse Perstempo Survey".

31   D.K. Orthner, *Family Impacts on the Retention of Military Personnel.* Paper presented at the Military Family Research Review Conference. Washington, D.C. (1990).

32   G. Vernez and G. Zellman, *Families and Mission: A Review of the Effects of Family Factors on Army Attrition, Retention, and Readiness* (Santa Monica, CA: RAND Corporation, 1987).

33   C. Bourg and M.W. Segal, "The Impact of Family Supportive Policies and Practices on Organizational Commitment to the Army," *Armed Forces & Society,* Vol. 25 (1999), 633-652.

34   M.A. White, H.G. Baker, and D.A. Wolosin, *Quality of Life in the Marine Corps: A Comparison Between 1993 and 1998.* (San Diego, CA: Navy Personnel Research and Development Center, 1999).

35   Robert Sadacca, Rodney A. McCloy, and Ani S. DiFazio, *The Impact of Army and Family Factors on Individual Readiness* (ARI Research Report 1643). (Alexandria, VA: U.S. Army Research Institute for the Behavioral and Social Sciences, 1993).

36   Jason Dunn and Robert Morrow, "Should I Stay or Should I go? Attrition Questionnaire Revision Project – Phase 1 Findings," Sponsor Research Report 2002-09 (Directorate of Human Resources Research and Evaluation, Ottawa, Ontario, Canada, 2002).

37   Leora N. Rosen, Linda Z. Moghadam, and Mark A. Vaitkus, "The Military Family's Influence on Soldiers' Personal Morale: A Path Analytic Model," *Military Psychology,* Vol. 1 (1989), 201-213.

38   M. Villeneuve, T. Dobreva-Martinova, G. Little, and Rena Izzo, "Military Unit Effectiveness and Readiness: A Theoretical Framework," Paper presented at the Human in Command Conference, Breda, The Netherlands. (June, 2000).

39   Mady Wechsler Segal, "The Military and the Family as Greedy Institutions," *The Armed Forces & Society*, Vol. 1 (1986), 9-38.

40   Kerry Sudom and Sanela Dursun, *The Relationship Study: Qualitative Findings.* (Centre for Operational Research and Analysis, Defence R&D Canada: Ottawa, Canada, 2006).

41   K. Myklebust, "The Impact of Family Issues Throughout the Deployment Cycle: The Human Dimension of Operations Project," Technical Note 99-3 (Director Human Resources Research and Evaluation, Department of National Defence, Ottawa, Ontario, Canada, 1999).

42   Daphne Spain and Suzanne M. Bianchi, *Balancing Act: Motherhood, Marriage, and Employment Among American Women* (New York: Russell Sage Foundation, 1996).

43   Bruce W. Eagle, Edward W. Miles, and Marjorie L. Icenogle, "Interrole Conflicts and the Permeability of Work and Family Domains: Are There Gender Differences?" *Journal of Vocational Behaviour*, Vol. 50 (1997), 168-184.

44   J.H. Pleck, "Paternal Involvement: Levels, Sources, and Consequences," in M.E. Lamb (Ed.), *The Role of the Father in Child Development* (New York: John Wiley & Sons, 1997), 66-103.

45   Pleck, "Paternal Involvement".

46   Lolita M. Burrell, Gary A. Adams, Doris Briley Durand, and Carl Andrew Castro, "The Impact of Military Lifestyle Demands on Well-Being, Army, and Family Outcomes," *Armed Forces & Society*, Vol. 33 (2006), 43-58.

47   Carl Andrew Castro, Amy B. Adler, and Thomas W. Britt, eds. *Military Life: The Psychology of Serving in Peace and Combat; The Military Family* (Westport, CT, Praeger Security International, 2006).

48   L. B. Hammer, J. C. Cullen, G. C. Marchand and J.A. Dezsofi, "Reducing the Negative Impact of Work-family Conflict on Military Personnel: Individual Coping Strategies and Multilevel Interventions," in C. A. Castro, A. B. Adler and T. W. Britt, Eds.), *Military life: The Psychology of Serving in Peace and Combat.* Vol. 3. The Military Family (Praeger Security International: Westport, Connecticut, 2006), 220-242.

49   Sanela Dursun, "Adaptation of Canadian Forces Members and their Spouses to the Demands of Military Life: The Role of Social and Organizational Support," Unpublished doctoral dissertation, Carleton University, Ottawa, Canada, 2009).

CHAPTER 11

THE IMPACT OF SPOUSAL EMPLOYMENT ON MILITARY PERSONNEL CAREER DECISIONS

JASON DUNN, SAMANTHA URBAN and ZHIGANG WANG
Director General Military Personnel Research and Analysis
Department of National Defence, Canada

INTRODUCTION

Social trends over the past decade, such as the rising number of dual-income families, have driven military spouses[1] to expect or want to be gainfully employed should they choose. Moreover, dual-income families are now the norm for a variety of reasons ranging from the requirement to pay bills to both spouses wanting a sense of fulfilment after attaining educational goals.[2] As a Canadian Forces member states:

> Dual-income families lose money on postings. Your spouse often has a hard time finding employment when you move, especially in small places like this one. Why take a posting when you know you're going to lose money on your house and lose $35,000-$50,000 because your partner can't find work?[3]

Research conducted on CF personnel and their families has demonstrated that some of the greatest factors affecting military personnel retention are family-related.[4] Aspects of military life such as postings, deployments and time away can influence the well-being of all family members. In particular, such aspects of military life can make it difficult for the spouses of military personnel to obtain and maintain employment. While there has been extensive research conducted by TTCP nations and allies on military families, this chapter places emphasis on Canadian research. Specifically, it examines the impact of spousal employment on military personnel career decisions.

PREVIOUS RESEARCH[5]

Spousal employment has been identified as a key factor for CF personnel when making career decisions. It has been found that the impact of military life on spousal employment and income was a source of considerable dissatisfaction for CF personnel.[6] In particular, the negative financial impact of being posted was identified as well as the negative impact that postings had on spousal careers and/or spousal ability to find suitable employment. It has also been found that conflict with the career of a spouse was an important reason for CF personnel choosing to leave the military.[7]

A study, based on open-ended data from the Canadian Forces Attrition Information Questionnaire-Revised (CFAIQ-R), provided further confirmation of the above findings.[8] Within this study, military personnel indicated that as a result of spousal employment, they had been forced to make a choice between being separated from their spouses (e.g., going on Imposed Restriction), asking their spouses to make career sacrifices, or leaving the military. Similarly, in their work on PERSTEMPO[9], Dunn, Ford and Flemming state that in general, "today's military family is much less portable, that is, that families [are] no longer traditional (e.g., male breadwinner) and that family considerations … often [outweigh] career considerations".[10]

Although complications arise as a result of military requirements and military life, there is a need for compromise within military families. In relation to employment, it is argued that spouses cannot be "too independent of one another, and must be flexible and willing to compromise at times".[11] In terms of CF personnel employment and that of their spouse's, compromises need to be made when a couple realizes that both cannot "simultaneously advance their careers".[12] In some cases, the couple might agree to let the member advance his/her career, while the spouse will have his/her turn later. However, this principle of equity can become problematic when personnel are posted.[13] While a posting may be a "good move" that may result in a promotion or other career benefits for military personnel, there may be costs for the families. The possibility that spousal careers would need to be refocused or changed as a result of difficulties in finding employment in their field is one such example.

Research has suggested that issues related to spousal careers and employment must be considered in accordance with changes in the CF, such as recruiting standards.[14] As noted, if all officers are required to have an undergraduate degree, it is likely that their spouses will also be similarly educated. Thus, "if the CF intends to attract the 'best and the brightest', how long can the organization realistically expect spouses to forego their career aspirations?"[15] Spouses may be willing to accommodate a few postings, but there may come a time when spouses will no longer be willing to accept the costs to their careers; an issue that may have a subsequent impact on the stay or leave decisions of CF personnel. As such, being perceived as an "employer of choice" is more likely to have an impact that extends well beyond the career of CF personnel.[16]

CURRENT RESEARCH – SPOUSAL/PARTNER EMPLOYMENT AND INCOME PROJECT

Given the potential organizational impacts, in October 2008, Chief Military Personnel (CMP) and Director General Military Personnel Research and Analysis (DGMPRA) initiated the CF Spousal/Partner Employment and Income (SPEI) project. The overall aim of the SPEI project was to gather data on the employment status and income of CF spouses and the key research questions included: a) What is the employment status and income of CF spouses vis-à-vis comparable groups? and b) What are the employment experiences of CF spouses?

The SPEI is currently in Phase Three[17] which consists of the analysis of data from the *Fall 2008 Your-Say Regular Forces Survey* (YSS) and the *2008 Quality of Life Among Military Families: A Survey of Spouses/Partners of CF Members* administered between November 2008 and March 2009.[18] The objective of Phase Three is to attempt to understand how aspects of military life impact the employment status and income of CF spouses. For the purposes of this chapter, specific questions from the YSS were examined to illustrate how spousal employment may impact military personnel career decisions regarding postings, promotions and attrition.

PRIORITIZATION OF MILITARY AND SPOUSAL CAREERS

In general, the data provided some indication that spousal employment may potentially impact military personnel decisions in relation to their careers. For instance, 16.9% of CF personnel believed that they had made career sacrifices as a result of their spouse's employment. Additionally, approximately 18% of CF personnel agreed that they were unhappy as a result of balancing their career needs with the career needs of their spouses. In terms of career prioritization, from this point forward in their careers, 28.1% of CF personnel agreed that their spouse's career was of a higher priority than their own. As a CF member states:

> My wife gave up her career for a decade to maintain our home for the eight months of the year I was at sea, and then to follow me around and out of Canada on three postings. This is now her time to work in her career field and my time to support her. Any posting I take is with the goal of family and spousal work stability remaining the priority.

POSTINGS AND SPOUSAL EMPLOYMENT

Findings indicated that although spousal employment may not have been as much of a motivating factor for CF personnel when contemplating postings in the past, it is now being given more consideration. For instance, Figure 11.1 illustrates that a small percentage of CF personnel surveyed (5.3%) reported that they had refused a previous posting as a result of their spouse's employment. A higher percentage (20.8%) indicated that they would refuse their next posting as a result of their spouse's employment.

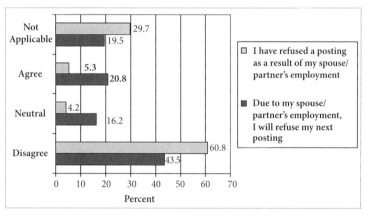

FIGURE 11.1: Previous and Future Posting Refusal Due to Spousal Employment

PROMOTIONS AND SPOUSAL EMPLOYMENT

Data were also examined relating to CF personnel refusing promotions. Figure 11.2 demonstrates that only 1.3% of CF personnel surveyed reported refusing a previous promotion as a result of their spouse's employment. A higher percentage (8.3%) indicated that they would refuse their next promotion due to their spouse's employment. Compared to the findings on posting refusal, it could be hypothesized that CF personnel are not as willing to sacrifice individual promotions for their spouses' employment.

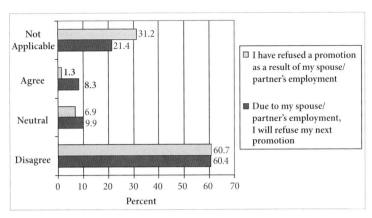

FIGURE 11.2: Previous and Future Promotion Refusal Due to Spousal Employment

To what extent have the following factors influenced your decision to leave the CF?	Considerable Influence
A desire to stay in one place	55.9%
My physical/psychological well-being	54.2%
Retirement	42.8%
A lack of work/family balance	38.7%
Lack of options for flexible work practices and career breaks	38.7%
Lack of career opportunities for spouse/partner	29.0%
My spouse/partner would prefer that I leave the CF	26.9%
Due to my spouse/partner's job/career	26.9%
Family responsibilities (e.g., caring for aging parent)	18.9%
Lack of family support systems	17.1%
Dissatisfaction with CF housing services	11.0%
Family isolation/lack of social support	10.1%
Dissatisfaction with relocation services	8.9%
Lack of education opportunities for my spouse/partner	7.2%
Lack of suitable childcare services	5.7%
Complications resulting from being a dual-service couple	0.3%

TABLE 11.1: "Considerable Influence" Factors for Leaving the CF

FACTORS INFLUENCING ATTRITION DECISIONS

While posting and promotion refusal due to spousal employment should be a concern for any military organization, of greater consequence is personnel attrition. Table 11.1 demonstrates factors that have considerable influence[19] on CF personnel decisions to leave the organization. While not among some of the top reasons, more than a quarter of CF personnel sample cited "lack of career opportunities for spouse/partner" (29%) and "due to my spouse/partner's job/career" (26.9%) as having considerable influence.

CONCLUSION

When the data above are examined collectively, it is clear that family considerations such as spousal employment are impacting the career decisions of military personnel in different ways. While emphasis in this chapter has been placed on posting and promotion refusal, as well as motivating factors for leaving the CF, further research is required to understand how spousal employment may influence additional career decisions. For instance, are military personnel more likely to refuse a posting if a promotion is not involved? Are they likely to accept a posting at the expense of their spouse's career if it involves a promotion? By further understanding the family lives of military personnel, senior leaders are able to ensure that proper policies and programs are in place to support them. Such policies and programs not only assist in maintaining morale, but are also beneficial in the retention of personnel.

ENDNOTES

1   For the remainder of this chapter, the word "spouse" will refer to and have the same meaning as "spouse/partner".

2   Julie Coulthard and Jason Dunn "Canadian Forces Spousal/Partner Employment and Income Project: Research Framework and Methodology," Director General Military Personnel Research and Analysis Technical Memorandum 2009-012 (Department of National Defence, Ottawa, Canada, 2009).

3   Jason Dunn and Robert Morrow, "Should I Stay or Should I Go: Attrition Questionnaire Revision Project – Phase 1 Findings," Sponsor Research Report 2002-09 (Director Human Resources Research and Evaluation, Department of National Defence, Ottawa, Canada, 2002), 8.

4   Karine Pépin, Kerry Sudom, and Jason Dunn, "Your-Say: Quality of Life," Defence Research Development Canada Centre of Operational Research and Analysis Technical Memorandum 2006-41 (Department of National Defence, Ottawa, Canada, 2006).

5   This literature review originates from Coulthard & Dunn (2009). Consult reference for further details on studies mentioned in this chapter, as well as additional Canadian (and American) research relating to military families.

6   Dunn and Morrow, "Should I Stay or Should I Go".

7   Rosemary O. Parker, "Officer Attrition Related to Terms of Service," Technical Note 9/91 (Canadian Forces Personnel Applied Research Unit. Ottawa, Canada, 1991).

8   David A. Jenkins, "Voluntary Attrition from the Canadian Forces: Qualitative Analysis of Data from the Revised Canadian Forces Attrition Information Questionnaire (CFAIQ-R)," Sponsor Research Report 2003-15. (Director Human Resources Research and Evaluation. Department of National Defence, Ottawa, Canada, 2003).

9   PERSTEMPO refers to the sum of the demands made by military service upon individual members (deployment load, time away, and workload).

10   Jason Dunn, Kim Ford, and Steve Flemming, "PERSTEMPO Qualitative Data: CF Member Focus Group Findings," ORD Technical Report 2005/09 Directorate of Strategic Human Resources. (Department of National Defence, Ottawa, Canada, 2005), 40.

11   Kerry Sudom and Sanela Dursun, "The Relationship Study: Qualitative Findings," Defence Research Development Canada Centre of Operational Research

and Analysis Technical Report 2006-36. (Department of National Defence, Ottawa, Canada, 2006), 11.

12   Sudom and Dursun,"The Relationship Study".

13   Deborah Norris, and Jason Dunn, "Healthy Family/Relationship Functioning: The Development of a Preliminary Model," Defence Research Development Canada Contract Report 2005-03. (Department of National Defence, Ottawa, Canada, 2005).

14   Johanna Ewins, "CF Household Survey," Reaction Research Report 00-1. Director Human Resources Research and Evaluation. (Department of National Defence, Ottawa, Canada, 2000).

15   Ibid., 41.

16   Ibid.

17   Phase One included a literature review and the development of the project methodology (Coulthard & Dunn, 2009). Phase Two included an analysis of data obtained from Statistics Canada using the 2006 long-form Census (Dunn, Urban & Wang, 2010).

18   Jason Dunn, Samantha Urban, and Zhigang Wang, "Spousal/Partner Employment and Income (SPEI) Project: How Do Canadian Forces Spouses Compare?" Director General Military Personnel Research and Analysis Technical Memorandum 2010-028 (Department of National Defence, Ottawa, Canada, 2010).

19   For this table, the "considerable influence" and "very considerable influence" response categories were merged together. In order to respond to these items, YSS respondents must have answered "yes" to the item, "Do you intend to leave the CF within the next three years?"

CHAPTER 12

SURVEYS: UNDERSTANDING THE MEASUREMENTS THAT INFORM DECISION-MAKING

WING COMMANDER EMMA DAVIS
New Zealand Defence Force

ELIZABETH EDGAR and ANNE BRACKLEY
United Kingdom, Ministry of Defence

INTRODUCTION

Within the enduring context of operational demands, competition for resources and talent, and need to achieve excellence, senior leaders need reliable information to guide and inform evidence-based planning and decision-making. Workforce intelligence provides part of the picture but this is greatly enhanced with the addition of high quality and robust survey data.

Employee surveys are widely used by organizations, including the military, in an effort to understand what it is that motivates people and which factors are critical to improving organizational effectiveness. Amongst the TTCP nations, organizational surveys have been used for many years to gather data from personnel to explore and monitor attitudes and perceptions and also identify and address key challenges.

Within the military a large number of surveys are conducted, ranging from the regular continuous attitude and exit surveys to one-off surveys which are designed to explore specific issues. Recent examples of these include deployment-related studies and family surveys. In order to provide valuable insight into what service members in our respective nations think, believe, feel and do, surveys ask personnel to report their opinions, attitudes, beliefs and behaviours regarding topics related to strategic HR, attraction and recruitment, selection, duty of care and force management.

With the popularity and prominence of surveys then, how do we ensure surveys are in fact delivering useful and meaningful workplace intelligence? This chapter provides guidance on best practice for conducting surveys and outlines the key issues that need to be considered to maximize the benefits of organizational surveying.

SURVEYS AND HR MANAGEMENT

In the context of HR management, questionnaire surveys are an efficient and effective tool for reaching a large or geographically dispersed group of people in an objective and minimally intrusive manner. A questionnaire survey is distinguished from a poll by the use of a sample. That is, the respondents are not selected indiscriminately or are only those who volunteer to participate, but rather, the sample is scientifically determined so that each person in the population will have a measurable chance of selection and the chances of ensuring a full representation of the total population is enhanced. This means the results can be reliably projected from the sample to the larger population. The intention therefore is not to describe the particular individual who responds, but to obtain an overall picture of the population being researched.

It is often the case that personnel surveys are carried out in a highly complex, real-life setting and it may be necessary to adapt the scientific approach accordingly. For example, the need to evaluate the effects of environmental factors such as policy changes may only be recognized after the event. Sometimes it will be possible to identify and survey the equivalent of control groups, but in most instances it is unlikely that a control group will exist. A partial solution to this issue is to gather baseline data where available against which future results can then be benchmarked and contrasted.

Nevertheless, embarking on any survey process requires a substantial commitment to the structured activities involved across the organization from both senior leadership and participants. Where surveys are conducted in accordance with best practice, and any limitations in their design are recognized, they will provide a valuable means of obtaining relevant data in a systematic and standardized fashion. Conversely, if good practice is compromised then the survey data could be unreliable and findings misleading.

DESIGNING AND USING QUESTIONNAIRES

In designing a survey tool, researchers must be able to demonstrate that they have taken into account theoretical and best practice principles in the design of their questionnaires and study methodology. An initial step, where relevant, should be to conduct a literature review to ensure the research is informed by previous findings and experience. The results of focus groups and interviews with personnel and Subject Matter Experts can also provide useful information in the design of questionnaire surveys.

Questionnaires and their individual items should be designed to ensure they draw out the information sought from the study. This sounds basic. However, some questions do not perform as expected at times and some questions could be superfluous to the topic of interest. Ideally, the items will have certain statistical properties when tested and can be shown to have relevance to the subject. The structure of the items and response scales should also be designed with data analysis in mind to avoid analysis resulting in unnecessary ambiguity. It is also important that where respondents provide free comments on a questionnaire, that these are analyzed and considered as part of the analysis and reported results of the survey.

It is necessary to pilot questionnaire surveys with an appropriate sample to identify any confusion with language, terminology or instructions and identify changes that make the survey more user-friendly and easier to complete.

Lastly, there are different methods by which a survey questionnaire can be administered. Contemporary technology has made the administration of surveys easier and more efficient and this is increasingly becoming the primary method of administration amongst TTCP nations. However, personnel's access to technology can be a barrier and some respondents may still prefer more traditional forms of interaction (i.e., paper-based questionnaires). We are still learning about some of the characteristics of e-surveys and how they may affect response rates. For example, the ease of electronic surveying may have contributed to over surveying some individuals, which, in turn, could contribute to declining response rates through a reluctance to complete any survey.

RESPONSE RATES

For leaders and decision-makers, it is important that surveys provide reliable and robust information. Confidence in the results of surveys can easily be undermined if the response rate is low or responses come from an unrepresentative sample of the population. Concern exists that non-respondents may have markedly different attitudes from respondents and, therefore, means the results may not provide an accurate picture of the population. Low response rates can also damage the credibility of the survey, because survey sponsors often use response rates as an indication of a survey's quality.[1]

Research has found declining response rates in public opinion polls, academic, organizational survey research and United States military research. For example, in the U.S. Navy, the top three reasons for non-response were a belief that surveys have no impact, general apathy towards surveys and survey length. Studies have also indicated the following reasons as pertinent: over surveying; the size and formal structure of the organization, high work demands; and lack of perceived benefit to respondents.[2]

In a review of studies published in leading management journals, average response rates have been reported as follows: 64% in 1975, 56% in 1985; and 48% in 1995.[3] In addition, Lamerson reported that response rates on military postal questionnaires administered by TTCP countries declined during the 1990s and continue to decline.[4] A TTCP collaborative document also identified that all of the TTCP nations experienced degrees of falling response rates, complaints of survey fatigue and perceptions that the results are not used.[5]

In a review of the literature, researchers identified studies that show a positive correlation between response rate and the following factors: education, writing ability, sex, age, occupation level and home ownership.[6] The experience of the TTCP nations also shows that officers consistently have a higher response rate than non-commissioned ranks.

Research has also investigated whether the answers provided by respondents and non-respondents on U.S. Quick Polls were equivalent, and found that overall a clear and consistent pattern of differences amongst completers and non-completers was not found.[7] However, officers who completed the survey did display higher organizational commitment than non-responders.

Other research has reported that personnel considered visible survey-based action more important than feedback when evaluating a survey's utility.[8] Visible action also had an impact on personnel's willingness to complete future surveys. Other initiatives that may be used in an effort to increase response rates include communication strategies, timing the survey administration wisely, reminder notices and the use of incentives.

There are a variety of reasons why people do not respond to surveys, but it is vital, in order to maximize response rates, to demonstrate that the survey results make a difference, provide participants with feedback and ensure that surveys are well designed and not too lengthy. Unfortunately, there is no gold-standard for response rates. However, researchers and stakeholders need to understand whether the population is well represented by the respondents and the results are consistent with other sources of information.

DATA ANALYSIS AND REPORTING

It is beyond the scope of this chapter to provide detailed guidelines on data analysis and reporting. However, when interpreting the results from a survey there are some key considerations to keep in mind which will provide information on the strength and relevance of the findings.

For example:

- Take into account the response rates, particularly for the targeted sample or sub-group you are most interested in;

- Note the sample sizes and profiles as these will determine the extent of any inferences and generalizations that can be made based on the survey data;

- Examine the statistical significance of effects and differences compared to only focusing on descriptive results. It is also useful to be aware that statistical significance should be interpreted appropriately where large samples are involved as very small effects may reach significance. The use of effect size calculation should be advocated when the data allow for it;

- Note any limitations of the data or research in either the methodology or respondent-related limitations; and

- Interpret the results with consideration to contextual information relating to local, organizational and national changes and events.

THE NEED FOR CONSENT

Whilst the requirements for ethical approval may vary across nations, there is normally a professional requirement to ensure those we are asking to be involved in a study or data capture exercise participate voluntarily and are not coerced. This is important not just from a research ethics perspective, but also because data elicited through coercion may not be the most reliable and could lead to misleading results. To try to avoid this, consent to participate is sought from participants. Consent to participate in a survey is elicited in different ways across nations and studies. In some cases, the fact that personnel have responded is taken as implicit consent. In other cases, personnel are informed that in responding to the survey are they are also providing evidence of their consent or they might be asked to complete a specific consent form. Regardless, there is an onus on the study sponsor to ensure participants are responding freely.

FINAL WORDS

In a pervasive climate where change and improvement is imperative to effectiveness, where leaders and policy developers require robust evidence to support their decisions, it is important to have trust in the processes used to capture employee attitudes. Well-conducted HR research is an essential component of human resource strategy and provides confidence to decision-makers in the development and implementation of HR programs. It is crucial to know when to trust in the measures and to understand the caveats associated with findings resulting from this type of real world research. Only by understanding the strengths and any limitations of the measurements can decisions leading to organizational improvement be fully informed.

ENDNOTES

1   Carol E. Newell, Paul Rosenfeld, Rorie N. Harris, and Regina L. Hindelang, "Reasons for Non-response on U.S. Navy Surveys: A Closer Look," *Military Psychology,* Vol. 16, No. 4 (2004), 265-276. (Edwards *et al.*, 1997, cited in Newell *et al.*, 2004)

2   Newell *et al.*, "Reasons for Non-response".

3   Ibid.

4   Cheryl Lamerson, "TTCP/hum/01/10: Survey Issues Across TTCP Nations" (September 2001).

5   Stephen Eyres, TTCP HUM TP3 Collaborative Paper: On the problem of "Over Surveying", A Collation of Opinions Among TP3 Nations (2006).

6   Newell *et al.*, "Reasons for Non-response".

7   Carol E. Newell, Kimberly P. Whittam, and Zannette A. Uriell, *Non-response on U.S. Navy Quick Polls* (2010).

8   Lori Foster Thompson and Eric A. Surface, "Promoting Favourable Attitudes Toward Personnel Surveys: The Role of Follow-Up," *Military Psychology*, Vol. 21 (2009), 139-161.

CONTRIBUTORS

Dr. **Jane M. Arabian** earned her B.A in Psychology at Connecticut College and her graduate degrees at the University of Toronto in Experimental Psychology. She is currently the Assistant Director for Enlistment Standards in the Accession Policy Directorate, Office of the Secretary of Defense. Dr. Arabian is responsible for planning and formulating policy on military enlistment standards pertaining to aptitude and education standards. She provides Research & Development oversight for the DoD aptitude testing programs, including the ASVAB Career Exploration Program, offered primarily to secondary school students. Dr. Arabian has over twenty-five years of government service and is the recipient of the Defense Medal for Exceptional Civilian Service. She is a Fellow of the American Psychological Association (APA), and past president of APA's Society for Military Psychology. Dr. Arabian served as the department's representative on The Technical Cooperation Program, Panel on Military Human Resources (TP3), from 1993-2010.

Anne Brackley MA, MSc, C.Psychol, AFBPsS, is an organizational psychologist who served as a senior member of the Royal Air Force (RAF) Occupational Psychology Team. In that role she conducted myriad studies related to RAF personnel, and she is well know for her innovative morale risk monitoring technique, which provided the ability to track changes in the morale and attitudes of RAF personnel during periods of substantial organizational change. Also known as the "RAF Pulse Survey", the technique employs frequent collection of key personnel metrics, and the ability to analyze data quickly and provide real time feedback to military leaders on the affects of organizational change on personnel well-being and effectiveness.

Wing Commander **Emma Davis** joined the Royal New Zealand Air Force as a military psychologist in 1993, having completed a Master's of Science in Psychology in 1990 at the University of Canterbury. Wing Commander Davis has enjoyed a number of appointments throughout New Zealand working in the areas of aviation psychology, assessment and selection, training development, organizational development and psychological support to operations. Since 2006, Wing Commander Davis has held the appointment of Director of Defence Psychology with the New Zealand Defence Force (NZDP). Wing Commander Davis has represented the NZDF as the National Leader for TP3 Military Human Resource Issues since 2007.

Jason Dunn is a defence scientist and team leader of the CF Family Research Team in the Personnel and Family Support Research Section of the Director General Military Personnel Research and Analysis within Canada's Department of National Defence, Ottawa.

Dr. **Sanela Dursun** is Director of the Research Section, Personnel and Family Support in DGMPRA at DRDC. Her research interests focus on: the impact of military lifestyle demands on the mental health and quality of life of members and their families; optimal length and frequency of operational deployments; family violence, etc. She has served as a member of TTCP TP3 panel and is currently a member of the Scientific Review Panel for the Millennium Cohort Family Study, Deployment Health Research. She received a Master's degree in social psychology and a PhD in health psychology from Carleton University.

Elizabeth Edgar is a Chartered Occupational Psychology who has researched and advised on defence personnel issues since 1996. She currently works as a Personnel Capability Advisor for the UK's Defence Science and Technology Laboratory (Dstl) which draws on and addresses a diversity of military personnel issues; from selection of specialist roles to support to families. Part of her current role involves capturing requirements; ensuring the methodological robustness of research proposals; and providing technical assurance. She is an Associate Fellow of the British Psychological Society and has taught psychology and research methods on various courses including Diploma in Aviation Safety for military officers; academic courses for pre-undergraduates; and a "delivering good research" course for Dstl.

Professor (Major) **Gerard Fogarty** is a Professorial Research Fellow in the Community and Organizational Research Unit at the University of Southern Queensland, Toowoomba, Australia. He completed his PhD on the structure of human intelligence at the University of Sydney in 1984 and moved to his present university in 1988. He is a Fellow of the Australian Psychological Society, a member of its College of Sport and Exercise Psychology, and a highly-published researcher in the fields of intelligence and cognition, organizational psychology, human factors, and sport psychology. Professor (Major) Fogarty joined the Australian Defence Force as a research consultant in 2008.

Dr. **Tonia Heffner** is a Team Leader in the Personnel Assessment Research Unit at the U.S. Army Research Institute for the Behavioral and Social Sciences. She received a PhD in Industrial/Organizational Psychology from the Pennsylvania State University in 1997 and a MS in Human Factors and Industrial/Organizational Psychology from Wright State University in 1992. She is President of the American Psychological Association's Division 19 (Military Psychology). Dr. Heffner's primary research focus is selection, classification, and promotion systems for soldiers and non-commissioned officers and she has numerous presentations and publications on these topics. Her current research focuses on longitudinal validation of non-cognitive assessments for selection and classification of new soldiers.

Melinda Hinton holds a Bachelor of Science (Hon) majoring in psychology from the University of Wollongong and held lecturing positions in cognitive psychology, psychometrics and statistics. She joined Defence as a research psychologist with the Psychology Research and

Technology Group in 2004 and became the Assistant Director of Psychometrics and Data Management in 2007. She has extensive experience in test design and administration, and development of military personnel selection systems. She is currently the Aviation Psychology and Safety Analyst for the Human and System Performance section of Defence Aviation and Air Force Safety.

Major **E. James Kehoe**, PhD, was raised and educated in the United States. He came to Australia in 1977 to take up an academic appointment at the University of New South Wales, where he is now Professor of Psychology in experimental and organizational psychology. He is also a reservist in the Australian Army Psychology Corps. He is posted as a consultant to the Head of Corps and has lectured in the first appointment course for specialist officers at the Australian Royal Military College.

Stephen Okazawa attended the University of British Columbia in Vancouver, Canada receiving Bachelor's and Master's degrees in Electro-Mechanical Engineering. His Master's thesis work was in the fields of medical robotics and real-time image processing. In 2004, he joined Defence Research and Development Canada and began working in the area of personnel operational research. His research has focused on modelling and simulation methodologies for military human resources management and logistics. He leads a team responsible for the development of new technology for large-scale military HR simulations. He is a member of an international technical cooperation panel on Workforce Modelling and Analysis.

Chad Ian Peddie is a Research Associate in the Personnel Selection and Development Program of the Human Resources Research Organization. He graduated with both a Bachelor's degree in psychology and a Master's degree in industrial/organizational psychology from George Mason University. He has conducted research in employee selection, organizational demography, diversity training, workplace discrimination, and occupational health psychology. His work has been published in peer-reviewed journals, book chapters, and presented at national conferences.

Dr. **Alla Skomorovsky** is a team leader for the Conditions of Service Team in the Personnel and Family Support Research Section, DGMPRA at DRDC. Her research interests focus on: the role of personality in the mental health of CF members; the impact of military life style demands on the quality of life of military families; coping with family violence; and stress and resilience. She has also been teaching psychology at the Royal Military College of Canada and personality topics at Carleton University for several years. She received a PhD in social psychology from Carleton University.

Dr. **Kerry Sudom** completed her PhD in psychology at Carleton University, Ottawa, and joined the Department of National Defence as a Defence Scientist in 2005. Currently, Dr. Sudom conducts scientific research and analysis to support improving the health and well-being of CF members. Her main areas of research include the health, quality of life, and economic outcomes of transition from military to civilian life; health and fitness trends among military personnel; and psychological resilience. She has also conducted research on the impacts of military life on families of Canadian Forces personnel.

Jamie Swann, (at the time of this writing), was a Research Psychologist working within the Psychology Research and Technology Group Australia Department of Defence. As part of the Personnel Selection Research section, he was involved in the design and review of psychometric instruments and selection systems for numerous ADF jobs, including technical trades, Joint Terminal Attack Controller and musician. Before this position he had previously worked on other research projects at Defence in the areas of mental health and alcohol and other drugs. He has since left Defence and currently conducts safety and recovery research for WorkSafe Victoria.

Brian Tate received his doctorate in Industrial/Organizational Psychology from Pennsylvania State University in 2009. After working as a Research Psychologist at the U.S. Army Research Institute for the Behavioral and Social Sciences, he currently works for Personnel Decisions Research Institutes as a Human Capital Consultant. His experience and education have primarily been in personnel selection, performance appraisal, and job analysis. He has published and presented works in these areas as well as in leadership, training and development, and individual differences.

Samantha Urban is a defence scientist and member of the CF Family Research Team in the Personnel and Family Support Section of the Director General Military Personnel Research and Analysis within Canada's Department of National Defence, Ottawa. She received her Master's Degree in Sociology in 2005 from Queen's University (Kingston). Her recent research focus has been on military spousal employment, relocation and recreation/leisure programs.

Angela Vearing works at the Department of Defence in Canberra, in the area of strategic personnel research. She has recently completed a Master's of Organizational Psychology through Monash University, where her research interests included identifying the personal and job-related predictors of sickness presenteeism.

Dr. **Zhigang Wang** is a defence scientist and member of the CF Family Research Team in the Personnel and Family Support Research Section of the Director General Military Personnel Research and Analysis within Canada's Department of National Defence, Ottawa. He received his PhD in social psychology from Carleton University in 2007. His recent research focus has been on military family issues.

Jennifer Wheeler is a registered psychologist and commenced work at the Department of Defence in 2001. Jennifer was a Senior Research Psychologist within the Psychology Research and Technology for seven years, and an Australian representative on TTCP Technical Panel 3 between 2004-2010. Her current position is Director – Navy Psychology Policy within Navy Health Services. Jennifer has a Master of Science Degree (University of Canberra) and Master in Management and Strategy (University of NSW). In 2007, Jennifer attended the Australian Command and Staff College (ACSC), and obtained the qualification of ACSC (joint).

GLOSSARY

ACISS	Army Communications and Information Systems Specialist
ACME	Arena Career Modeling Environment
ACSC	Australian Command and Staff College
ADF	Australian Defence Forces
AFQT	Armed Forces Qualification Test
ANAV-RAM	Air Navigator Resource Allocation Model
APA	American Psychological Association
ASVAB	Armed Services Vocational Aptitude Battery
BARS	Behaviourally Anchored Rating Scales
BOTC	Basic Officer Training Course
BRT	Basic Recruit Training
CAT	Computer-Adaptive Testing
Cat.	Category
CAT-ASVAB	Computer-Adaptive Testing – Armed Services Vocational Aptitude Battery
CBT	Computer-Based Testing
CF	Canadian Forces
CFAIQ-R	Canadian Forces Attrition Information Questionnaire-Revised
CHRC	Canadian Human Rights Commission
CMP	Chief Military Personnel
CPTM	Cost-Performance Tradeoff Model

GLOSSARY

DGMPRA	Director General Military Personnel Research and Analysis
DoD	Department of Defense
DRDC	Defence Research Development Canada
Dstl	Defence Science and Technology Laboratory (U.K.)
FFM	Five Factor Model
FOR	Frame of Reference
GAO	Government Accountability Office
GED	General Education Diploma
GMA	General Mental Ability
HR	Human Resources
HRM	Human Resource Management
IBT	Internet-Based Testing
IM	Impression Management
INBT	Intranet-Based Testing
IP	Internet Protocol
IQ	Intellectual Quotient
ITC	International Test Commission
IT&E	Individual Training and Education
JPM	Job Performance Measurement
KSAOs	Knowledge, Skills, Abilities and Other Characteristics
MARS	Managed Readiness Simulator

NCM	Non-Commissioned Member
NCO	Non-Commissioned Officer
NZDF	New Zealand Defence Force
O*NET	Occupational Information Network
PAQ	Position Analyses Questionnaire
PP	Paper-and-Pencil
PR	Project Report
RAM	Random Access Memory
SME	Subject Matter Expert
SPEI	Spousal/Partner Employment and Income Project
TM	Technical Memorandum
TP3	Technical Panel 3
TR	Technical Report
TSD-PI	Trait-Self Descriptive Personality Inventory
TTCP	The Technical Cooperation Panel
U.K.	United Kingdom
U.S.	United States
USAF	United States Air Force
WWW	World Wide Web
WOSB	War Officer Selection Board
YSS	Your-Say Regular Forces Survey

INDEX

A

applicants   vii, 4, 13, 41, 51-59, 67, 71, 78, **81** *notes*, 85-90, 97-101, 105-108, **110** *notes*, **111** *notes*

aptitude   39-43, 50, 53-56, 67, 68, **70** *notes*, 102, **109** *notes*, 165

assessment centres   viii, 50, 51, 56, 85, 86, 88, 89, 91-93, **95** *notes*, **96** *notes*

attrition   **36** *notes*, 39, 41-44, 46, **47** *notes*, 79, **144** *notes*, **145** *notes*, 148, 150, 153, **154** *notes*

attitude surveying   157, 158, 160

Australian Defence Force (ADF)   50, 58, 61, 76, 167, 169

B

behaviourally anchored rating scales (BARS)   124-126

behavioural dimensions   87

behavioural/social learning approach   72

biographical data measures   51

biological approach   72

C

Canadian Forces (CF)   i, v, **36** *notes*, **37** *notes*, 76, 77, **81** *notes*, **82** *notes*, 137-140, **146** *notes*, 147-153, **154** *notes*, **155** *notes,* 166, 169, 170

cognitive approach   73

commitment   58, 127, 128, 137, 138, 141, **144** *notes*, 159, 161

J

job analysis vii, 1-5, 8-15, **16-18** *notes*, 56, 88, 119, 125, 128, 170

job knowledge 51, 55, 66, 119, 123

job performance 6, 13, 14, 40-44, 46, **47** *notes*, 54-58, **59** *notes*, 65, 66, **69** *notes*, 75, 76, 79, **80** *notes*, 86, 88, 91-94, 114-121, 127

L

low stakes tests 100

M

managed mode 101, 107

military family v, vii, 133, 138, 141, **143-146** *notes*, 148, 170

modelling vii, 1, 9-12, 19, 20, 22, 23, 34, 35, **36** *notes*, **37** *notes*, 168

N

neuroticism 73-77, 79, **81** *notes*

O

objective measures 73, 120, 121, 123

occupational analysis **18** *notes*

on-line testing viii, 97

open mode 101

organizational citizenship behaviour 114-117, 121, 128, **129** *notes*

organizational commitment 138, **144** *notes*, 161

overt tests 57

P

peer rating 51, 57, 118, 122

performance appraisal/rating 1, 14, 58, 113, 114, 117-124, 126, 127, **128-131** *notes*, 170

personality viii, 4, 6, 50, 54-57, **59** *notes*, **60** *notes*, **65** *notes*, **66** *notes*, **69** *notes*, **70** *notes*, 71-79, **80-83** *notes*, 98, 101, 106, 107, **111** *notes*, 169

personality-oriented tests 57

personnel selection **15** *notes*, 50, **59** *notes*, 77, **83** *notes*, 85, 86, 91, 92, 113, 129, 168-170

postings 147-151

promotion 4, 13, 14, 22-25, 27, 29, 73, 79, 91, 113, 117, 122, 123, 141, 149-153, 167

psychoanalytical approach 72

Q

questionnaires 8, **17** *notes*, 55, **110** *notes*, **111** *notes*, 159-161

R

recruit i, v, vii, 19, 23, 24, 26, 39-44, 46, **47** *notes*, 61, 62, 76, 77, **81** *notes*, 97, 140, 141

referee report 57

response rates 160-162

retention **36** *notes*, 41, 46, 137, **142** *notes*, **144** *notes*, 147, 153

S

scenario 21, 22, 25, 26, 28, 30, 33, 35, 43, 53, 54

self-report 76, 77, 100

10

INDEX

V

W